"Andy Crouch has done it again! *Strong and Weak* is an intellectually insightful, socially relevant and prophetically passionate book that shows us how to multiply our power to create a world where people from every tribe and nation can flourish and reach their full God-given potential. I love it!"

Brenda Salter McNeil, Seattle Pacific University, author of *Roadmap to Reconciliation*

"*Strong and Weak* gives biblical substance to the call to stewardship in the broadest sense—stewardship of self, vocation, gifts, resources and suffering. The stewardship of suffering is perhaps the most critical work of a leader, and often the most overlooked. This will become required reading for our leadership and development work."

Lisa Slayton, president, Pittsburgh Leadership Foundation

"God's Word focuses so much on the interplay between weakness and strength—as well as other opposites that drive us toward the greatest opportunities to flourish. All of discipleship seems to center around these opposites. When we experience poverty, we comprehend the riches that God generously bestows on us. When we experience helplessness, we recognize the might of his strength! Andy Crouch's excellent book gives insight into understanding all this more clearly."

Ravi I. Jayakaran, director, Community Transformations, e3 Partners, senior associate for integral mission, Lausanne Movement

"This book challenged me to think authentically as a leader and to bring my real self into the work of leadership. Andy Crouch offers a simple yet profound framework that examines the important relationship between authority and vulnerability—and how various combinations can either help or hinder human flourishing. This roadmap exposes the all-too-easy pitfalls of withdrawal and exploitation while reminding us that it is in vulnerability and suffering that strength dwells. *Strong and Weak* is an empowering guide for anyone who seeks to live against a culture of safety and into a life of meaningful risk and flourishing."

Jena Lee Nardella, cofounder, Blood:Water, author of *One Thousand Wells*

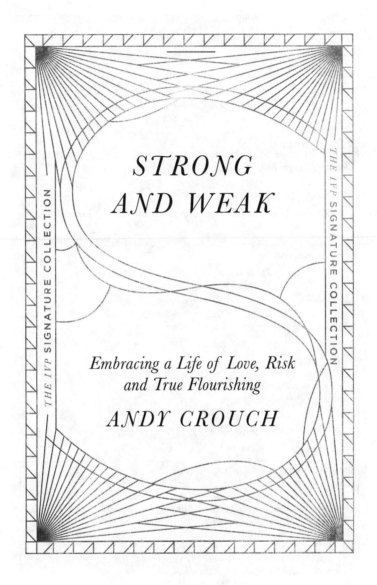

STRONG AND WEAK

Embracing a Life of Love, Risk and True Flourishing

ANDY CROUCH

ivp

An imprint of InterVarsity Press
Downers Grove, Illinois

InterVarsity Press
P.O. Box 1400 | Downers Grove, IL 60515-1426
ivpress.com | email@ivpress.com

©2016 by Andy Crouch

InterVarsity Press® is the publishing division of InterVarsity Christian Fellowship/USA®. For more information, visit intervarsity.org.

Published in association with Creative Trust Literary Group, 210 Jamestown Park, Suite 200, Brentwood, TN 37027, creativetrust.com.

Scripture quotations, unless otherwise noted, are from the New Revised Standard Version of the Bible, copyright 1989 by the Division of Christian Education of the National Council of the Churches of Christ in the USA. Used by permission. All rights reserved.

While any stories in this book are true, some names and identifying information may have been changed to protect the privacy of individuals.

The publisher cannot verify the accuracy or functionality of website URLs used in this book beyond the date of publication.

Cover design: David Fassett
Interior design: Beth McGill

ISBN 978-0-8308-4709-9 (paperback) | ISBN 978-0-8308-4710-5 (digital)

Printed in the United States of America ∞

Library of Congress Cataloging-in-Publication Data
Names: Crouch, Andy, author.
Title: Strong and weak : embracing a life of love, risk, and true flourishing / Andy Crouch.
Description: Downers Grove : InterVarsity Press, 2016. | Includes bibliographical references.
Identifiers: LCCN 2015040195 (print) | LCCN 2015042608 (ebook) | ISBN 9780830844432
    (hardcover : alk. paper) | ISBN 9780830899289 (eBook)
Subjects: LCSH: Success–Religious aspects–Christianity. | Love–Religious aspects–Christianity. |
    Vulnerability (Personality trait) | Risk taking (Psychology)–Religious aspects–Christianity. |
    Control (Psychology)–Religious aspects–Christianity.
Classification: LCC BV4598.3 .C755 2016 (print) | LCC BV4598.3 (ebook) | DDC 248.4–dc23
LC record available at http://lccn.loc.gov/2015040195

29 28 27 26 25 24 23 22 | 13 12 11 10 9 8 7 6 5 4 3 2 1

In memory of Steve,

joyfully

Contents

1

Beyond the False Choice

Two questions haunt every human life and every human community. The first: *What are we meant to be?* The second: *Why are we so far from what we're meant to be?*

Human beings have an indelible sense that our life has a purpose—and a dogged sense that we have not fulfilled our purpose. Something has gone wrong on the way to becoming what we were meant to be, individually and together.

The first question exposes the gap in our own self-understanding, our half-formed sense that we are meant to be more than we know. How can we have such a deep sense of purpose but find ourselves unable to easily name or grasp that purpose? Yet this is the human condition.

The second question exposes the gap between our aspirations and our accomplishments, between our hopes and our reality, between our reach and our grasp. If the first question gives voice to our greatest hopes, the second brings to the surface our deepest regrets. Having both great hopes and great regrets is also, alas, the human condition.

In this book I offer a way of answering both of these questions. It's simple enough to explain in a minute or two of conversation, or in a page or two of a book—it's coming up in just a few pages, and you'll grasp its essence almost immediately. You'll see it in action in your friendships, your workplace, your family and your favorite TV show or movie—you'll find it in the pages of Scripture and in the most mundane moments of day-to-day life. You'll see it in the most horrifying contexts of injustice and exploitation, and in the most inspiring moments of compassion and reconciliation.

Many simple ideas are *simplistic*—they filter out too much of reality to be truly useful. This one is not, because it is a particular kind of simple idea, the kind we call a *paradox*. It holds together two simple truths in a simple relationship, but it generates fruitful tension, complexity and possibility. I've come to call it the *paradox of flourishing*.

"Flourishing" is a way of answering the first great question, *What are we meant to be?* We are meant to flourish—not just to survive, but to thrive; not just to exist, but to explore and expand. "*Gloria Dei vivens homo,*" Irenaeus wrote. A loose—but by no means inaccurate—translation of those words has become popular: "The glory of God is a human being fully alive." To flourish is to be fully alive, and when we read or hear those words something in us wakes up, sits up a bit straighter, leans ever so slightly forward. To be fully alive would connect us not just to our own proper human purpose but to the very heights and depths of divine glory. To live fully, in these transitory lives on this fragile earth, in such a way that we somehow participate in the glory of God—that would be flourishing. And that is what we are meant to do.

Every paradox requires that we embrace two things that seem like opposites. The paradox of flourishing is that true flourishing requires two things that at first do not seem to go together at all. But in fact, if you do not have both, you do not have flourishing, and you do not create it for others.

Here's the paradox: flourishing comes from being both strong and weak.

Flourishing requires us to embrace both authority and vulnerability, both capacity and frailty—even, at least in this broken world, both life and death.

> Flourishing comes from being both strong and weak.

The answer to the second great question—*Why are we so far from what we're meant to be?*—is that we have forgotten this basic paradox of flourishing, which is the secret of being fully alive. Actually, we haven't just forgotten it, as if we had misplaced it absentmindedly. We've suppressed it. We've hidden it. We've fled from it. Because we fear it.

I used to think that what we feared was vulnerability—the "weak" part of the paradox. But in the course of writing this book and talking with many others about the paradox of flourishing, I've realized that we fear authority too. The truth is that we are afraid of both sides of the paradox of flourishing—and we especially fear to combine them in the only way that really leads to real life, for ourselves and others.

This book is about how to embrace the life for which we were made—life that embraces the paradox of flourishing, that pursues greater authority and greater vulnerability *at the same time.*

But most of all, this book is about a picture, the simplest and best way I know to explore the paradox of flourishing. It's really just a sketch, the kind of thing you can draw on a napkin, but it will give us plenty to think about for the rest of this book (see figure 1.1).

It's one of my favorite things: a 2x2 chart.

THE POWER OF THE 2X2

There's nothing I find quite as satisfying as a 2x2 chart at the right time. The 2x2 helps us grasp the nature of paradox. When used properly, the 2x2 can take two ideas we thought were opposed to one another and show how they complement one another.

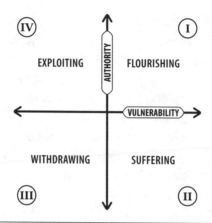

Figure 1.1

The world is littered with false choices. The leadership writers Jim Collins and Scott Porras talk about "the tyranny of the OR and the genius of the AND." Should products be low cost *or* high quality? Whom do managers serve, their investors *or* their employees? The most transformative companies manage both. Are we the products of our nature *or* our nurture? They are not opposites—they have to go together.

The Christian world has its own versions: Is the mission of the church evangelism and proclamation *or* is it justice and demonstration? Are we supposed to be conservative *or* radical, contemplative *or* active, set apart from the world *or* engaged in the world? Or take the topic that almost generated the first great biblical 2x2 chart. Is the life of the Christian about faith *or* works? ("Show me your faith apart from your works, and I will show you a 2x2 chart of my faith and works"—James 2:18, my take on the original Greek!) Then you'll be ready for the ultimate question: Was Jesus of Nazareth human *or* divine? Was he Son of Man *or* Son of God?

In all these cases, what we need is not a linear "or" but a two-dimensional "and" that presses us to see the surprising connections between two things we thought we had to choose between—and perhaps even to discover that having the fullness of one requires that we have the fullness of the other.

One of the best examples comes from studies of effective parenting—the kind of parenting that produces children who display self-confidence and self-control. Which is better, to be a strict, demanding parent who sets firm boundaries, or a responsive, engaging parent who interacts with their children with warmth and compassion? If you were a parent, where on this spectrum would you want to be (see figure 1.2)?

Put the question this way and most parents will lean one

Figure 1.2

way or the other. Some will quote Proverbs—"spare the rod, spoil the child"—and opt for firmness (see Proverbs 13:24). Others will quote Paul—"Fathers, do not provoke your children to anger"—and opt for warmth (see Ephesians 6:4, Colossians 3:21).

Both are right.

Firmness and warmth, it turns out, are not actually opposites. They can go together—in fact, they must go together for children to flourish. Their relationship is much better shown with a 2x2 (see figure 1.3).

Map firmness and warmth this way, and you quickly discover that *either* one, without the other, is poor parenting. Firmness without warmth—authoritarian parenting—leads

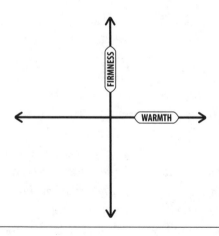

Figure 1.3

eventually to rebellion. Warmth without firmness—indulgent parenting—leads eventually to spoiled, entitled brats.

In fact, there aren't just two ways to be a bad parent—there are three! The worst of all is parenting that is neither warm nor firm—absent parenting (see figure 1.4).

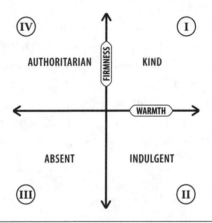

Figure 1.4

There is a difference, it turns out, between being nice and being kind. "Nice" parenting drifts down to the bottom right, settling for easy, warm feelings without ever setting high expectations. Kind parenting manages to be clear and firm while also tender and affectionate. Psychologists call it *authoritative* parenting rather than *authoritarian*. The best parenting, in our 2x2, is up and to the right.

There are a few more insights hidden in this simple diagram.

I've numbered the quadrants using Roman numerals I to IV, starting with the ideal quadrant up and to the right and continuing around clockwise—in the same order and direction we'll consider them for the next four chapters. Consider the line from the top left to the bottom right, from quadrant IV (Authoritarian) to quadrant II (Indulgent), from firmness without warmth to warmth without firmness.

Remember our one-dimensional line with warmth on the left and firmness on the right? In practice, if that is your mental model of parenting, you'll end up becoming either authoritarian (firmness without warmth) or indulgent (warmth without firmness). The IV-II line describes the line of *false choice*—the world we often think we live in (see figure 1.5). It describes our default way of thinking about

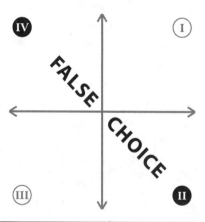

Figure 1.5

how the world works—at least when we are limited to a linear model.

Because neither authoritarian nor indulgent parenting produces healthy results, they tend to generate and reinforce one another. Grow up in an authoritarian home, and you may well react by being an overly indulgent parent. Grow up with indulgence, and you may well overcorrect toward strictness when your own children come along. Much of the dysfunction of our lives comes from oscillating along the line of the false choice, never seeing that there might be another way.

One other observation: There is one quadrant that really is the worst of all. It's quadrant III (Absent), the quadrant of withdrawal and disengagement. Authoritarian parents may not meet their children's need for affection, but at least they provide structure. Indulgent parents may not provide structure, but at least they create an environment of acceptance and affirmation. But absent parents leave two voids in their children's lives, not just one. There's something about the Absent quadrant that is uniquely damaging—the total opposite of the Kind quadrant.

You could sum it up this way: We tend to think that our lives have to be lived along the line of false choice, the IV-II line. But actually the deepest question of our lives is how to move further and further away from quadrant III (Absent) and more and more fully into quadrant I (Kind).

The III-I axis is the one that matters the most—the one that leads from a life that is not worth living to the life that really is life. And that, in a nutshell, is what this book is about.

THE PARADOX OF JESUS

No human being ever embodied flourishing more than Jesus of Nazareth. No human life (let alone death) ever unleashed more flourishing for others. And precisely for this reason, no other life brings the paradox of flourishing so clearly into focus. In the life of Jesus we see two distinct patterns that can seem impossible to reconcile.

On the one hand, consider the bookends of his life on earth. He was born an infant, utterly dependent like every other human being. He ended his life on a Roman cross, was buried and descended to the dead. One of Christianity's oldest texts puts it this way:

> Though he was in the form of God,
>   [he] did not regard equality with God
>   as something to be exploited,
> but emptied himself,
>   taking the form of a slave,
>   being born in human likeness.
> And being found in human form,
>   he humbled himself
>   and became obedient to the point of death—
>   even death on a cross. (Philippians 2:6-8)

On the other hand, there were Jesus' three years of flourishing public ministry, the culture-making effects of which resound through history and throughout the world—the most consequential life ever lived. Christians believe that this very Son of Man and Son of God now sits at the right hand of the Father, truly the world's Lord, and sends his Spirit of power to equip us to live his life in the world. To quote the very next line of that same ancient text: "Therefore God also highly exalted him and gave him the name that is above every name" (Philippians 2:9). Indeed, Jesus himself told his first followers that they would do even greater things than he himself had done (John 14:12).

But how can these two callings—to humility and to boldness, to death and to life, to submission to the worst the world can do and to reigning with Christ over the world—possibly coexist? What do they mean for those of us who have some scope of choice and action—those of us who have been granted privilege and power? What do they mean for those who live at the cruelest edges of the world, in settings of implacable injustice and oppression? Is there really any Christlike way to exercise leadership within our broken

> How can these two callings—to humility and to boldness, to death and to life, to submission to the worst the world can do and to reigning with Christ over the world—possibly coexist?

human institutions all the way up to (or down to) the church itself? What would be the specific practices we could adopt to live in ways that bear the true image and bring lasting flourishing?

We need a way to hold these two seemingly opposing facets of Jesus' life, and our calling, together—a way to navigate this complexity without being overwhelmed. Which means we need a 2x2 chart, of course.

THE DIMENSIONS OF POWER

I'm sure you see it coming already—the two dimensions of Jesus' life, his vulnerability in dependence and death on the one hand, his authority in his earthly ministry and his heavenly exaltation on the other hand, can easily start to seem like linear alternatives. Exaltation or humiliation? Ascension or crucifixion? Miracles of healing, deliverance and even resurrection, or, "My God, my God, why have you forsaken me?" The empty tomb or the cross? The only way to hold them together is a 2x2 (see figure 1.6).

Some of us will instinctively identify with, or aspire to, the "vulnerability" dimension. Perhaps that is the reality of our lives—it is, eventually, the reality of every mortal life. It may be the reality of the community or family into which we were born, making us keenly aware of the limits of our power and the precariousness of our circumstances. Or we may aspire to identify with vulnerable people and places.

From those places and with those people, we look at Jesus and see vulnerability. Jesus identified with the vulnerable in his birth, life and death. Whether we identify with vulnerability or aspire to it, Jesus is there.

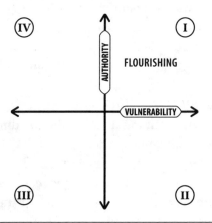

Figure 1.6

On the other hand, others of us identify with, or aspire to, authority. We have been told we can make a difference in the world; we've been given opportunities for creativity and leadership. Other people respond positively when we suggest a course of action. Maybe we've invested substantial amounts of our time and money (maybe our parents' money) in gaining authority in the form of training and certificates and degrees. We look at Jesus and see authority—as early as age twelve in the temple, engaging powerfully with the scribes; standing up in his hometown synagogue and boldly proclaiming himself as the fulfillment of the prophet's vision; confounding Pilate and the Jewish leaders even when he was in chains; breathing on his disciples after his resurrection and giving them his Spirit, telling them they were now commissioned to go out into the whole world with his authority. Whether we identify with authority or aspire to it, Jesus is there.

When we identify with one dimension or another, it's easy to become impatient with people who emphasize the other one. I worked in a campus ministry on an Ivy League campus where we emphasized the Christian call to "downward mobility," to use one's privilege and power as an opportunity to serve the materially and spiritually poor. One day an African American student confronted me. "When I came to college," he said with some frustration, "my entire community held a prayer service and laid hands on me to commission me to go to Harvard. And now you want me to tell them that I'm just coming back to the hood to work for a nonprofit ministry?" His community had commissioned him for authority—power and position in parts of the culture where they had historically been absent or underrepresented. Who was I to tell him not to stay on that path?

What I was missing, at that point in my life, was a 2x2 conception of authority and vulnerability—the possibility that the journey of Christian discipleship, and true power, would involve not just a progression toward one or the other, but toward both at the same time. Such a conception would not simply authorize my student to leave his vulnerability behind and pursue privilege and power, but it also did not authorize me to ignore his (and his community's) legitimate pursuit of flourishing and the authority that flourishing requires.

This book is my long overdue answer to that student. First we will examine the four possible combinations of authority and vulnerability on that 2x2 diagram. Properly combined, authority and vulnerability lead to flourishing (chapter 2). But when either one is absent—or even worse, when both are missing—we find distortions of human beings, organizations and institutions. We find *suffering*, *withdrawing* and *exploiting* (chapters 3, 4 and 5)—which in their most virulent forms become poverty, apathy and tyranny. They don't always appear to be that bad—poverty can look like mild disempowerment, apathy can look appealingly like safety, tyranny often seems like mastery. In another layer of complexity, it will turn out that all of us inevitably spend time in each of these three quadrants, and God's grace is real and available in them all. But none of them is the fullness of what we are made for, the life that is really life.

So how do we move up and to the right on this 2x2 chart?

Surprisingly, rather than simply moving pleasantly into ever greater authority and ever greater vulnerability, we have to take two fearsome journeys, both of which seem like detours that lead away from the prime quadrant. The first is the journey to *hidden vulnerability* (chapter 6), the willingness to bear burdens and expose ourselves to risks that no one else can fully see or understand. The second is *descending to the dead* (chapter 7), the choice to visit the most broken corners of the world and our own heart. Only once we have made these two fateful journeys will we be the kind of people who can be entrusted with true power, the power that moves *up and to the right* (chapter 8) and brings others who have been trapped in tyranny, apathy and poverty along with us.

In the book *Mountains Beyond Mountains*, the renowned public health physician Paul Farmer tells his biographer, Tracy Kidder, "People call me a saint and I think, I have to work harder. Because a saint would be a great thing to be."

I think Farmer is entirely right that a saint would be a great thing to be. The saints are, ultimately, the people we recognize as fully alive—the people who flourished and brought flourishing to others, the ones in whom the glory of God was most fully seen. There really is no other goal higher for us than to become people who are so full of authority and vulnerability that we perfectly reflect what human beings were meant to be and disclose the reality of the Creator in the midst of creation. "Life holds only one tragedy," the French Catholic Léon Bloy wrote, "not to have been a saint."

But becoming a saint is about quite a bit more than "working harder"—or perhaps better put, it's about a great deal less. If you have some inkling, like Farmer, that a saint would be a great thing to be, and if you also have some inkling that you never could work hard enough to actually become one, you're on the path to true flourishing.

2

FLOURISHING

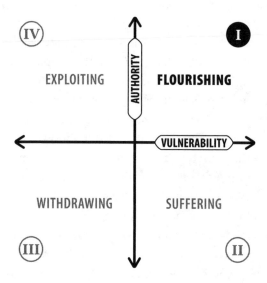

Flourishing is something both we and our neighbors seek and want. *Flourishing* captures Jesus' statement of his own life's purpose in John 10:10, "I came that they may have life, and have it abundantly." It echoes Paul's words to Timothy as that young man sought to pastor the wealthy in his congregation, urging him to lead them toward "the life that really is life" (1 Timothy 6:19). To be fully, abundantly, gloriously alive—this would be flourishing. What could we desire more?

But there is a danger here, and Paul understood it. To say that there is a "life that really is life" implies that there is a life that is *not* really life. You can be mistaken. You can miss it. You could possibly live your whole life without ever knowing what real life is. And Paul implies that the people most at risk for missing "the life that really is life" are the rich.

Since nearly every reader of this book possesses wealth that would have been unimaginable to Paul and Timothy, resources out of reach of most of the billions with whom we share the planet, Paul's warning should ring in our ears. If there is a life that is not really life, there is surely a flourishing that is not really flourishing. So perhaps we should remind ourselves what flourishing is *not*.

Flourishing is not the life we see portrayed in the commercial messages that have saturated the imagination of every resident of the mediated world—the unselfconsciously multicultural millennial tribes, the blissfully happy families with their responsible-yet-still-cool parents and cheeky-but-still-lovable kids, the youthful retirees on the weathered porch, all glowing in the warmth of the photographers' golden hour.

Flourishing is not health as we normally understand it.

There are people with profound physical and mental disabilities who flourish and make flourishing possible for others, while there are gyms full of people hitting their personal bests who are nonetheless not flourishing.

Flourishing is not the same thing as growth—the ubiquitous Southern weed we call kudzu grows, all right, but a roadside overgrown with kudzu is not flourishing.

Flourishing is not affluence. There can be flourishing among the materially poor, and there can be a debilitating spiritual sickness among the affluent.

Flourishing is not gentrification. There are flourishing communities that never appear on lists of the hippest neighborhoods, and a Whole Foods or a sudden influx of people carrying yoga mats is no guarantee of a flourishing neighborhood.

How do we know that flourishing is none of these things? Because the most influential human being in history was a Judean carpenter and rabbi who did not live in a gentrified neighborhood (although, to be fair, he did tell at least one person to pick up his mat). He was never noted for his physical appearance (in fact, he had "nothing in his appearance that we should desire him," see Isaiah 53:2). His circle of followers first expanded then dwindled as his mission reached its culmination—from curious crowds of thousands to a few steadfast and heartbroken women standing by his cross.

He lived the most exemplary human life possible, but it was not a life that looks like our affluence-addled picture of flourishing.

Define flourishing carelessly—define it hastily, instinctively, from a position of temporary power or privilege—and you will end up missing the real thing, or the real One.

You will miss Jesus—and you will also miss Angela.

ANGELA

Like all my sister Melinda's children, Angela, her third of four, was born in a plastic inflatable tub in the middle of their living room, attended by a midwife and surrounded by family—a scene that will give you some sense of my confident, resilient and countercultural sister. (My wife Catherine and I have preferred to experience the miracle of new life in, shall we say, more controlled environments.)

But the moment that Angela arrived in the world, the midwife's patient and cheerful coaching shifted suddenly to decisive urgency. I will never forget picking up the phone, three hundred miles away, and hearing my father's anguished voice as he struggled to say the words, "There's something wrong with the baby." By that time Melinda, her husband, Dave, the midwife and Angela were already speeding toward the regional hospital, half an hour's drive over mountain roads from their home.

There was indeed something wrong—one basic thing

wrong, it turned out, that led to many other things wrong. Angela, doctors determined after days of tests, had three copies of her thirteenth chromosome, a condition called trisomy 13. (The far more common condition called Down Syndrome involves an extra copy of the twenty-first chromosome—trisomy 21.) Some babies are born with a milder "mosaic" version of this condition that only affects some cells. In Angela's case, every cell had this debilitating extra set of instructions.

Many children with trisomy 13 die before birth; half of those born alive die within the first week. Trisomy 13 affects almost everything, for the worse, in a human body—from the unfused plates in Angela's skull that first alerted the midwife to her need for urgent medical attention, to the curled-in toes on her feet. It is so rare that even at the tertiary-care facility where she was cared for, most doctors had only heard of the condition, never seen it. When they did see it, their words were grim.

My brother-in-law still has the notebook where he tried to keep track of what the endless parade of specialists said in those first few frantic days. Early on he wrote down the phrase, "Incompatible with life." Yet eleven years later, Angela was still alive.

She could not meaningfully see or hear; she could not walk; she could not feed or bathe herself. She knew nothing of language. We could only guess what she knew or understood of her mother, her father, her grandparents, brother and sisters. Early on she would respond to voice and touch; in recent years, even as she had grown physically, she had for long seasons receded further into an already distant and un-knowable world.

Which leads to this question: Is Angela flourishing?

THE FLOURISHING OF THE VULNERABLE

If your definition of flourishing is the life held out for us by mass-affluent consumer culture, the obvious answer is that Angela is not flourishing—never has and never will. She cannot purchase her satisfactions; she cannot impress her peers; she cannot even "express herself" in the ways we think are so important for our own fulfillment.

But perhaps the question actually has things backwards. When Jesus was asked, "Who is my neighbor?" he told a parable that turned that question on its head, ending with the question, "[Who] was a neighbor to the man who fell into the hands of robbers?" (Luke 10:29, 36).

If we were to similarly turn the question of flourishing around, maybe we would be asking, "Who is helping Angela flourish?" We might be asking, "Who is flourishing because of Angela?" And even, "How can we become the kind of people among whom Angela flourishes and who flourish with Angela in our midst?"

Flourishing is not actually the property of an individual

at all, no matter how able or disabled. It describes a community. The real question of flourishing is for the community that surrounds Angela—her parents and siblings, her extended family, the skilled practitioners of medicine and education and nutrition who care for her, and in a wider sense the society and nation of which she is a citizen. The real test of every human community is how it cares for the most vulnerable, those like Angela who cannot sustain even a simulation of independence and autonomy. The question is not whether Angela *alone* is flourishing or not— the question is whether her presence in our midst leads us to flourishing *together*.

Then the question goes one step further. Is Angela helping us flourish? Is she the occasion of our becoming more fully what we were created to be, more engaged with the world in its variety and complexity, more deeply embedded in relationship and mutual dependence, more truly free?

The surprising answer is that precisely because of Angela's great vulnerabilities, because of the immense challenges that accompanied her into the world, a kind of flourishing is possible that would not otherwise exist. For ten years and counting,

> The question is not whether Angela *alone* is flourishing or not—the question is whether her presence in our midst leads us to flourishing *together*.

untold people have had the opportunity to serve Angela and her family with authority and with vulnerability. The medical teams who have cared for her from the earliest days have had to bring all their authority as physicians and caregivers to bear on her many vulnerabilities. But because her condition is so complex and all-encompassing, mere medical authority is by no means sufficient—everyone involved with Angela must also take risks, be willing to learn and discover that they were mistaken, be willing to open themselves to the reality that even the most effective medical care will only provide partial healing.

The only kind of power that can sustain Angela's life has to be up and to the right in our 2x2 diagram. Authority without vulnerability will not suffice. Neither will vulnerability without authority. The two together are what is needed. And these two together, I have come to believe, are the very heart of what it is to be human and to live for God and others.

If there is someone in your own life who has contributed in dramatic ways to your own flourishing—a parent, a teacher, a mentor, a friend—they almost certainly acted with authority in your life and exposed themselves to vulnerability as well.

If you have ever been part of a community that experienced some real measure of flourishing (a business, a church, a neighborhood, a sports team, a musical ensemble, a class)—some group of people who experienced a deep health and growth, among whom the vulnerable were welcomed and the strong were vulnerable—I suspect you'll find that among the characteristics of that community were high authority and high vulnerability. It's the way we were meant to live.

TRUE AUTHORITY

Think of authority this way: *the capacity for meaningful action.* When you have authority, what you do, or do not do, makes a meaningful difference in the world around you. Teachers and nurses have authority in the classroom and the hospital; plumbers have authority with pipes and landscapers have it with plants; pilots have authority with airplanes and librarians have it with books. When you have authority, you can ask, command, or even merely imply that something should be done, and it will be done. Not all authority, though, is about the ability to command or control. Sometimes it means knowing, or being known, in ways that set you free. An electrical engineer can read a circuit diagram that would stump the rest of us, understand how it works and see how to make it work better. If you have risen through the ranks of a business, you can walk into meetings and those present will already know your name, your character, your track record. You will be able to act in ways that you cannot act among strangers.

Authority requires that our action be *meaningful,* not just willy-nilly activity. I can idly pluck the strings on a guitar, but because I have never learned the guitar, my plucking has no real musical meaning or value. No one may be stopping me from picking up the instrument and plucking the strings, but I still do not really have the authority to play the guitar.

What makes action meaningful? Above all, meaningful action participates in a story. It has a past and a future. Meaningful action does not just come from nowhere, and it does not just vanish in an instant—it takes place in the midst of a story that matters.

Authority, at least for human beings, is always *limited*. The president of the United States has a great deal of executive authority within that nation, but none at all when visiting another country; and of course that capacity for meaningful action is conferred only for four years at a time, eight years at the most. Authority is limited not just in space and time, but to particular domains—the CFO of a firm has broad authority over the firm's accounting controls, but not generally over its advertising decisions, and he or she has no authority over the accounting practices of another firm.

Perhaps most importantly of all, true authority is always *given*. The capacity for meaningful action is not something we possess on our own. It is something others confer on us.

Without being given countless gifts—of language, of nurture, of love—by those who cared for us in our infancy and childhood, none of us would have the capacity to act meaningfully in the world. Without being continually affirmed and upheld in our capacity to act, none of us would be able to exercise whatever authority we have—as teachers, parents, pastors, presidents or coaches. Sociologists distinguish between "ascribed" authority and "achieved" authority—the kind that comes from a title or an inheritance versus the kind that comes from a history of successful action—but both come from outside ourselves. Authority, like flourishing, is a shared reality, not a private possession.

More Authority Than Any Other Creature

Human beings have far more authority than any other creature. Other creatures act, certainly, and even act with lasting effects, sometimes reshaping their environment in significant ways (as a beaver does when building a dam). But they do so in limited ways and always in a particular ecological niche. Human beings, on the other hand, have found ways to flourish and act meaningfully in nearly every ecosystem on the planet, from the steppes of Siberia to tropical rainforests—even, in modern times, to the continent of Antarctica. The first readers of the biblical command to "be fruitful and multiply, and fill the earth and subdue it" (Genesis 1:28) can only have had the faintest inkling of how truly human beings have been able to fulfill that call—and, as well, how terribly we have been able to abuse it.

Likewise, no other creature, at least in any way we can tell, acts *meaningfully* in the ways that human beings do— that is, acts as part of a grand and complex story about the world's origins and destiny and their place in it. There are other creatures on the continent of Antarctica, but none of them are pondering the history and destiny of our planet and cosmos in the way that the scientists are doing as they conduct experiments there. (Indeed, the fact that human beings will voluntarily travel to a land of constant subzero temperatures and no daylight for three months a year, just to *study* the world, is an extraordinary testimony to our desire for meaning.)

No other species has such a clear sense of responsibility for *other* species—what Christian theology calls *dominion*, the capacity and responsibility to act on behalf of the flourishing of the rest of creation. The psalmist of Psalm 8, having considered the vastness of the cosmos and human beings' smallness in the midst of it, then proclaims,

> Yet you have made them a little lower than God,
>   and crowned them with glory and honor.
> You have given them dominion over the works of
>   your hands;
>   you have put all things under their feet,

all sheep and oxen,
   and also the beasts of the field,
the birds of the air, and the fish of the sea,
   whatever passes along the paths of the seas.
     (Psalm 8:5-8)

This authority, uniquely ours as the image bearers of God, is a gift in every way. It does not come from our own autonomous selves—it is given by Another. And it is good. The sorrow of the whole human story is not that we have authority, it is the way we have misused and neglected authority. Our drive for authority—our sense of frustration when we are denied it or our sense of grief when we lose it—comes from its fundamental goodness.

So authority is *meant to characterize every image bearer*—even the most vulnerable. As infants, long before we could provide for ourselves in any way, we learned that we were capable of meaningful action. We emerged from the womb and instinctively sought to recognize a human face. We learned that others would give meaning to our cries.

Even my niece Angela has authority in this sense. Certainly her authority is limited—but as we have already seen, that is actually true for every human being. Like everyone's authority, Angela's capacity for meaningful action comes from the community around her. When she cries out with frustration, hunger or discomfort, others around her interpret those sounds and respond. They incorporate her actions, as unconscious and limited as they are, into a story, a shared reality with a past and a future. Angela's capacity for meaningful action is a gift, to be sure—one she cannot earn or sustain on her own. But that does not make it less real—that makes it true authority.

And Angela certainly has the other quality that makes us uniquely human, uniquely capable of bearing the divine image. The other thing that is essential for the exercise of true power is our vulnerability.

Two Kinds of Vulnerability

The way I will use the word *vulnerability* in this book is a bit different from its usage in America today, where it is often limited to personal and emotional transparency. We live in an age of oversharing. Ordinary people and celebrities disclose all kinds of seemingly shameful or incriminating details of their lives. Indeed, some people who have become celebrities simply through the sheer volume and extravagance of their self-disclosure are praised for their "vulnerability."

But this is not really what I mean by the vulnerability that leads to flourishing. Instead, think of it this way: *exposure to meaningful risk.* Sometimes emotional transparency is indeed a meaningful risk—but not always. For one thing, what was truly vulnerable and brave in one generation can become a key to success in another. When you can acquire fame, wealth and significant cultural power by frequently appearing on screen physically naked, nakedness can become less about the exposure that human beings fear and more about the "exposure" that every would-be celebrity needs—a currency of power, not of loss.

The vulnerability that leads to flourishing requires risk, which is the possibility of loss—the chance that when we act, we will lose something we value. Risk, like life, is always about probabilities, never about certainties. To risk is to open ourselves up to the chance that something will go wrong, that something will be taken from us—without knowing for sure whether that loss will come to pass or not.

> The vulnerability that leads to flourishing requires risk.

To be vulnerable is to be exposed to the possibility of loss—and not just loss of things or possessions, but loss of our own sense of self. *Vulnerable* at root means *woundable*—and any wound deeper than the most superficial scratch injures and limits not just our bodies but our very sense of self. Wounded, we are forced to become careful, tender, tentative in the way we move in the world, if we can still move on our own at all. To be vulnerable is to open oneself up to the possibility—though not the certainty—that the result of our action in the world will be a wound, something lost, potentially never to be gained again.

Here again we need the word *meaningful* to do its work. We are not talking about willy-nilly risk, putting ourselves in harm's way for no good reason. Nor are we talking about risking things we don't care whether we keep or lose, playing poker with chips that never have to be cashed in. True vulnerability involves risking something of real and even irreplaceable value. And like authority, true vulnerability involves a story—a history that shapes why we are choosing to risk and a future that makes the risk worthwhile but also holds the potential of loss coming to pass. When we expose ourselves to meaningful risk, we become vulnerable in the sense I will use the word in this book.

So emotional transparency *can* be meaningful risk—or it can be calculated manipulation. An already powerful person can use what seems like emotional honesty, even tears, to win followers, avoid confrontation or sidestep accountability. If you are in a setting where emotional transparency will almost certainly win you a hearing or undermine others' criticisms, to be emotionally transparent may indeed be the right thing to do. It may even be part of the proper exercise of your *authority*, a meaningful action that will contribute to your community's story. But it is not necessarily *vulnerable*.

NAKED CREATURES

The very first word of Patrick Lencioni's "business fable"

Getting Naked is *vulnerability.* His fable tells the story of a small but unusually successful consulting firm that is swallowed up by a larger and more conventional company. The secret of the smaller firm's success, it turns out, is vulnerability. Lencioni applies the vivid phrase "getting naked" to actions consultants can take in front of their clients that directly challenge three fears: fear of losing the business, fear of being embarrassed and fear of feeling inferior. It's a compact catalogue of the sources of authority in the consulting world: profit, prestige and a reputation for being smarter than anyone else. Even though Lencioni agrees that consultants need to be profitable, be well regarded and bring unusual insight to the table, his fictional narrator Jack discovers that achieving those goals actually requires putting them at risk— "getting naked" by exposing oneself to the possibility of losing them all. Jack learns to make honest but difficult observations about his clients' businesses—and perhaps more difficult, to be willing to ask "dumb questions" that reveal his own limits or ignorance.

Nakedness is a funny thing. Of all the creatures in the world, only human beings can be naked. By adulthood, every other creature naturally possesses whatever fur, scales or hide are necessary to protect it from its environment. No other creature—even naked mole rats or Mr. Bigglesworth, the hairless feline sidekick of Mike Myers's movie villain Dr. Evil—shows any sign, in its natural state, of feeling incomplete in the way that human beings consistently do. Only human beings live our whole lives able to return to a state that renders us uniquely vulnerable, not just to nature but to one another.

The unsettling truth is that just as human beings have more authority than any other creature, we also have more vulnerability than any other creature. We are not just born naked, we are born dependent, exposed in every conceivable way to the possibility of loss. For far longer than even our closest evolutionary relatives, after we are born we are dependent on others to nourish us, clean us and protect us. For many years we remain immature—unable to fully assert our authority competently in the world. (With the extension of adolescence in the modern world, that timespan keeps growing—Joseph and Mary presumably made their trip to Bethlehem when she was a teenager, but it's not until age twenty-five that you can freely rent a car from most companies in the United States and not until age twenty-six that parents must remove children from their health insurance plan. The length of time you can live in your parents' basement is continually being renegotiated upward as well!)

This is the essential human condition: greater authority *and* greater vulnerability than any other creature under heaven. Indeed, as the scholar Walter Brueggemann pointed out many years ago, the way the original man in

Genesis 2 recognizes the original woman as his suitable partner, after seeing so many other creatures that would never suffice, is with this outburst of poetry: "This at last is bone of my bones and flesh of my flesh" (Genesis 2:23). Bones—hard, rigid, strong. Flesh—soft, pliable, vulnerable. We image bearers are bone and flesh—strength and weakness, authority and vulnerability, together.

The same psalmist who celebrated human dominion over the creatures also was capable of looking up into the heavens and grasping what they meant for the significance, or insignificance, of our small and transitory lives: "When I look at your heavens, the work of your fingers, / the moon and the stars that you have established; / what are human beings that you are mindful of them, / mortals that you care for them?" (Psalm 8:3-4). Only a human being can fully grasp the meaning of that canopy of stars, of the infinitude of the Creator's life before and after our small lives—so only a human being can be so completely exposed to meaningful risk.

I have come to believe that the image of God is not just evident in our authority over creation—it is also evident in our vulnerability in the midst of creation. The psalm speaks of authority and vulnerability in the same breath—because this is what it means to bear the image of God.

When the true image bearer came, the "image of the invisible God" (Colossians 1:15), he came with unparalleled authority—more capacity for meaningful action than any other person who has lived. His actions all took their place within the story of Israel, the greatest of all shared histories, and they decisively changed the path of history and created a new and different shared future. And yet he, too, was born naked, as dependent and therefore vulnerable as any human being; and though the Western artistic tradition has placed loincloths over the uncomfortable truth of crucifixion, he died naked as well. He died exposed to the possibility of loss, not just of human life but of his very identity as the divine Son with whom the Father was well pleased. He was laid in the dust of death, the final and full expression of loss. And in all of this, he was not just Very Man but Very God.

What Love Longs to Be

As I was writing this chapter the makers of the GoPro line of cameras had their latest viral video hit. A helicopter drops the skier Cody Townsend at the top of a seemingly impossible, nearly vertical crevasse between two rock walls at the top of a snow-covered mountain. Thanks to the head-mounted camera, we follow him off the edge, plunging down through the narrow canyon and out, safely, just barely, onto the gentler slopes below.

It is terrifying. (One person who shared it online said that as he watched, he "tightened every orifice in sympathy.") It is also mesmerizing and exhilarating.

What makes this ninety-second video so compelling and compulsively shareable? It's the combination of authority and vulnerability—Townsend's complete command of the sport of skiing plus his willingness to stretch that competence to its absolute limit, to the point where there was the real possibility of loss. A video that showed authority without vulnerability might be impressive, but it would ultimately be boring; a video that showed gratuitous risk-taking without commensurate authority might well be good for a few laughs in the genre of "stupid human tricks," but it would not provoke astonishment, admiration and awe. What we truly admire in human beings is not authority alone or vulnerability alone—we seek both together.

When authority and vulnerability are combined, you find true flourishing. Not just the flourishing of the gifted or affluent, but the needy and limited as well. For my niece Angela to flourish, others will have to act meaningfully and place her own actions in a meaningful story. Indeed, if Angela's condition could be solved with a simple, technical medical procedure, perhaps all it would take to restore her health would be someone with medical authority. But her condition is too comprehensively challenging for that—it will

> What we truly admire in human beings is not authority alone or vulnerability alone—we seek both together.

never be "solved." So Angela's flourishing also depends on others being willing to put something meaningful at risk—the doctors charting an uncertain and difficult medical treatment, the caregivers who bear the difficulties and indignities of providing for a broken human body, and above all her parents choosing to love sacrificially, day after day, in the face of a most uncertain future.

In the end, this is what love longs to be: capable of meaningful action in the life of the beloved, so committed to the beloved that everything meaningful is at risk. If we want flourishing, this is what we will have to learn.

What we will have to unlearn, and be saved from, are our failures of authority, vulnerability or both—and that is the territory we now must explore.

3

SUFFERING

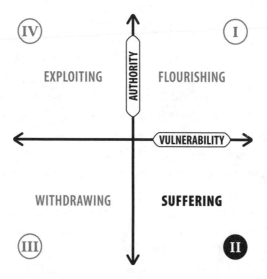

When did the topic of justice become important to you?" Gideon Strauss posed that question to two dozen people crammed into our living room one fall evening in Swarthmore, Pennsylvania. Some of us were there because we knew Gideon's remarkable personal story—

growing up Afrikaner in the last years of apartheid
South Africa, becoming deeply involved in that coun-
try's post-apartheid Truth and Reconciliation Com-
mission. Others were interested in his work with the
Center for Public Justice, an innovative think tank in
Washington, DC.

From my eleven-year-old daughter—perched on her
mother's lap for lack of chairs—to the gray-haired couple
from a nearby suburb, all of us took turns answering
Gideon's question. A few minutes earlier you could have
mistaken this gathering for a polite dinner party of reasonably diverse, prosperous professionals. But as we went
around the circle, as so often happens, the answers went
deeper and deeper, longer and longer.

Almost every answer to Gideon's question involved a
story of violence.

In this room of seemingly secure citizens of the United
States, there was hardly anyone who had not encountered
some kind of forceful violation of dignity that had shaken
their world, bruised their innocence and kindled a passion
for justice. That word *justice*, potentially so abstract and
distant, was in fact acutely personal. But for me one answer
came even closer to home.

Abby, an Asian American physician a few years younger
than me, had been invited by mutual friends. When her
turn came to answer Gideon's question, she began, "When

I was a girl my family moved to a suburb of Boston, Massachusetts, called Needham."

Needham! My family, too, had moved to Needham when I was thirteen years old. I came of age there, and it will always be home for me, though my parents moved away years ago. Abby was from my hometown. I barely restrained a delighted outburst as she continued her story.

"There was a convenience store named The Little Peach in Needham."

Yes, there was—down the street from the high school, right across from the Methodist church where I came to a living faith. My friends and I stopped at The Little Peach countless afternoons in my high school years. I enjoyed a pleasant wave of nostalgia (and a distinct memory of the taste of Orange Crush soda) as Abby went on.

"One day my dad needed to use the copy machine there, and he brought me along. I must have been seven or eight years old." I quickly estimated the years—that would have been my sophomore or junior year in high school.

"My father was born in China, and his English was poor. He had trouble figuring out how to get the copy machine to work. But he couldn't explain his problem to the owner of the store. The owner became furious with my father. He started mocking my dad's Chinese accent. Then he grabbed my father's papers, ripped them up and tossed them on the floor, and told us to get out of his store."

Abby paused. "I had always known my father as strong, kind and smart. I had never seen him humiliated like that in front of me. He was so ashamed—I was so ashamed. I didn't know what racism was before that day and what it could do to someone—but after that, I knew."

VULNERABILITY WITHOUT AUTHORITY

I never knew.

All those years, full of the joyous energy of adolescence, my friends and I—all of us "white" without ever giving it one moment's thought—had spilled out the doors of that little convenience store, sodas in hand. To us, racism was something that happened long before and far away, not under our noses, not at the copy machine I used a dozen times or more, not at the counter of The Little Peach.

For me, Needham was always about flourishing—the place where I came of age, discovered talents and ability, learned to pray and fell in love, was granted authority and discovered vulnerability. For Abby, it was the place where the violence of the world burst into the open, where her own father saw his authority ripped into pieces and thrown to the floor, his identity mocked and his weakness exploited. The place where an eight-year-old girl started a journey that would lead her, one day, to a circle of people, bruised by violence, seeking justice.

That afternoon in The Little Peach, eight-year-old Abby

discovered what it is like to live with vulnerability without authority. Authority, the capacity for meaningful action, has many sources. It comes from facility in a language—but immigrants trade their native tongue for one they learn with difficulty, if at all. It comes from citizenship in a nation and all the rights that come with citizenship— but many immigrants arrive with only provisional status, at best, in the new land. It comes from membership in an extended family, the deep knowledge of people and place that is only acquired over generations—immigrants give all that up the moment they step on the ship or plane that takes them away from their home. Immigration is such a drastic step that few would take it except in cases where the vulnerability of staying home, whether economic, political or cultural, is even greater than the vulnerability of trying to make a life and a living in a new home.

> That afternoon in The Little Peach, eight-year-old Abby discovered what it is like to live with vulnerability without authority.

Abby's parents had taken that step. And one of the most admirable things about the United States is how much authority they had in fact been able to acquire, in the form of economic and educational opportunities, by the time they arrived in Needham. But on that afternoon, Abby was rudely awakened to all the ways her parents lived with vulnerabilities she had not seen—how authority could be snatched out of her father's hand and ground spitefully underfoot. She had discovered the reality of life in the corner called Suffering.

DISCOVERING SUFFERING

None of us make it very far in life without spending time in this corner. Suffering can be the result of injustice and evil, but it touches even the most sheltered lives.

My friends and I in Needham knew little of the worst of the world, but suffering found us all the same. My friend Paul, head over heels in love with a girl named Janet, was summoned to the back of the library stacks junior year, where Janet told him she had tried to commit suicide the previous weekend. She was breaking up with him, she said, so he wouldn't have to deal with her depression. I knew nothing of this until six years later, when it spilled out in a conversation one summer day back from college, and Paul wept as uncontrollably as if it had happened yesterday. That same summer, one of my best friend's parents divorced, and I suddenly replayed my memories of their home in high school and realized that all those years his family had lived with toxic bitterness, as corrosive as any acid to the hope and confidence of their children.

I will never forget the first funeral I attended for someone my age, in the church across the street from The Little

Peach. Matt had been practicing with the freshman football team when he noticed unusual bruises from the gentlest of collisions. Four months later, he died from leukemia, and my friends and I sat in the overflow crowd in the vestibule of the church as we watched his parents walk in to the service. In his grief, his father looked to me like the strongest man in the world carrying the heaviest weight in the world on his shoulders. Out of nowhere, suffering had found him, and us.

All this happened to me, and around me, in one of the most protected corners of the world, in one of the most affluent places on the planet. (Even decades later, the wounds are deep enough that I have changed names and identifying details in this chapter out of respect for friends' privacy.) Wherever you come of age, suffering will come into your life earlier than you expected, in the form of risks you cannot manage and pain you cannot avoid, a room with no exit.

Ultimately, suffering—vulnerability without authority— is the last word of every human life, no matter how privileged or powerful. We will end our days, one way or another, radically vulnerable to others, only able to hope that they will honor our diminishment and departure with care and dignity. The authority we carefully store up for ourselves will evaporate slowly or quickly, over the span of decades—or over brunch.

ERIC AND KATE

Before I really talk with Eric and Kate for the first time, I can already make a rough guess of their status and occupations. Eric is athletic, handsome, in a suit with an open collar; Kate is dressed with the effortless panache that takes a great deal of effort. It's not hard to picture her on the paths along Boston's Charles River with the other early-morning runners (a more apt name for her Lycra-clad tribe than "joggers"). He works in finance; she works in marketing—they both live on Beacon Hill, Boston's neighborhood for young professionals with good jobs, good friends and good prospects.

They began dating, I find out, shortly before Eric started going to church. Eric is effusive in his newly discovered faith—Kate is more reserved. And yet you sense her opening up to the possibility that a loving God knows her and is seeking her, along with a growing wonder at the openness and generosity she has discovered among the followers of Jesus.

On Easter Sunday, a few months after we meet, Eric and Kate attend church and go out for brunch with friends. In the middle of the meal, Kate's head droops, and then her whole body goes limp. An ambulance rushes Kate, unresponsive, to the emergency room of Massachusetts General Hospital. By the time I get Eric's anguished email to a few Christian friends later that night, she is in the neurological intensive care unit.

On Monday morning, and every morning for the next week, I visit to support Eric and to pray with him as Kate's chest rises and falls with the mechanical rhythm of the life-support equipment. Her face is expressionless, pale, soft as with sleep. The hospital's chief of neurology takes over Kate's case and spends hours with the family and with attending physicians, interns and nurses at Kate's side. They have arrived at a diagnosis: a rare and undetected genetic condition has made Kate vulnerable, all her life, to a massive stroke. It could have happened years ago; it could have waited years longer. On Easter Monday, there is still some hope Kate might recover, at least partially. Over the coming days that hope dwindles. She will never open her eyes again. Late one afternoon, with her family around her, the doctors remove the equipment from her body and she is gone.

I attend the funeral in one of Boston's most affluent suburbs—not very different from my own home of Needham. The impeccably dressed mourners arrive in late-model SUVs, and I am reminded of how highly New England's elite value their control—control over slippery roads, over appearances, over emotions, over relationships. Kate's roommates give bewildered eulogies, grasping for profundity out of friendships born largely of carefree partying and the small trials of college life. The faith that she had just begun to explore hovers over a service that is hollow with grief.

At the graveside I am surprised to see the hospital's chief of neurology. He is perhaps sixty years old—he has cared for countless patients, has risen to the very top of his profession at one of the most prestigious medical centers in the world, and yet here he is at this young woman's grave, his face streaked with tears. He is shorter than I remembered from the hospital. He reaches up to embrace Eric and says, "I'm so sorry we couldn't save her."

THE PATHS TO SUFFERING

Of the four quadrants, Suffering is the one we least want to visit. And yet it is the only one I can be absolutely sure every reader of this book has experienced. You may or may not feel you have ever tasted the flourishing that comes from simultaneously experiencing great authority and great vulnerability; you may or may not have ever lingered in the withdrawal of having neither authority nor vulnerability; perhaps you have never had the opportunity to taste the tantalizing promise of authority without vulnerability. But without a doubt you have experienced vulnerability without authority, risk without options.

We suffer in the hospital waiting room, knowing that the

child or parent or friend who just was taken into surgery has taken everything we cherish in life with them—but also knowing that we can do nothing, beyond faithful waiting and prayer, to affect the outcome.

We suffer in romance, being on the receiving end of one of the worst and most cowardly inventions of the modern age, the breakup by text message. (Now *that* is vulnerability without authority!)

We even suffer in ambition, having sent off an application for a job or a place at university, all the documentation we could muster of our authority—but then having to wait weeks or months for a decision.

Indeed, sometimes suffering is simply the painful payoff of risking love in a broken world. This is the burden of Eric at Kate's grave, but it is also the burden of the chief of neurology at Mass General Hospital, with all his professional success and skill; it's the burden of the widower closing his wife's casket after fifty years of marriage; on a smaller but still very real scale, it is the burden of my friend grieving his breakup with Janet six years later.

But there is another path to suffering, one that has nothing to do with the risks that come with true flourishing. The other path is injustice—the spiritual and physical violence done by those who seek authority without vulnerability. Abby's father had done nothing to earn the violent contempt of the proprietor of The Little Peach, but

that man's distorted use of his petty power did damage all
the same—far more damage, surely, than any satisfaction
he gained from his display of superiority. One bleak day I
sat with my friend Jeremy the day after his divorce was fi-
nalized. His ex-wife had opted out of marriage with its demands for growth and transparency. It is surpassingly unlikely that she will end up happier in the long run, but the
damage has been done in their lives and the life of the
young daughter she left behind.

The most painful path to the quadrant called Suffering
is the human choice, at the very origins of the species, to
pursue Exploiting—to seek authority without vulnerability,
godlike power without God-like character. We are vulnerable without authority because our first parents sought
authority without vulnerability—and because their fallen
children seek it still.

GENERATIONS OF SUFFERING

Any experience of vulnerability without authority is painful,
but the deepest and most intractable examples of suffering
are communal and multigenerational. They involve whole
peoples who find themselves stuck in suffering, whole
communities with a shared painful history and a dismal
expected future.

This is not just a matter of financial deprivation. Even if
you are personally materially poor, if your community—

your family of origin, your ethnic group, your nation—has some measure of authority and can resist the worst of human vulnerabilities, you are at a much lower risk of true poverty. You are connected with others who can restore some measure of flourishing in your life.

Conversely, even if you are personally materially well-off, if your community is mired in suffering—if your parents, people and nation have known little for generations but enforced helplessness due to tragedy and injustice— then you are not free from the oppressive reality of suffering. And this kind of suf-

> The deepest and most intractable examples of suffering are communal and multigenerational.

fering is far deeper, and far less tractable, than the suffering all of us experience as individuals—because simply escaping it as an individual does nothing to change the fundamental systems of vulnerability without authority.

Sandra grew up in Ventura County in southern California, and she carries herself with the confidence that seems to be the birthright of children of those safe, sunny, endless suburbs, the confidence that carried her to university and into a professional career. Meeting her for the first time, I make a host of assumptions—almost all of which turn out to be wrong.

I assume that like so many young Americans, she can

largely chart her own course in life, choosing her college
major and career—when in fact, every one of these decisions has been discussed and debated and decided by her
whole extended family.

I assume she grew up knowing she would go to college.
In fact, no one in Sandra's family had ever gone to college.
For most of her childhood it was a distant and hazy dream.

I assume her parents worked hard to pay for her education—but in fact, Sandra's parents worked hard her
whole life at several jobs each, not to save money but to pay
for basic daily expenses.

I assume she grew up in a loving, stable home, which is
half true. Her family was generous and warm, but stability
was far beyond their grasp—because although Sandra was
born in the United States, her parents were not. They have
spent her whole life in the United States without legal
status. Early in her teens, translating from the Spanish that
is their only fully comfortable language to the English that
she speaks like the American native she is, she fully grasped
the reality: any hour, any day—at a routine traffic stop or
when a white Immigration & Customs Enforcement vehicle would pull up at the places where they held down
their informal, under-the-table jobs—they could in an instant be taken away from her, back to the land they left
before she was born.

Her family is part of the vast and complicated story of

undocumented immigration to the United States—a story of brave and hard-working people leaving homes of little opportunity and perilous violence to take back- and spirit-breaking work in American factories and fields. During Sandra's years in junior high school, a movement began to force the issue of these long-term, tax-paying residents and workers. Sandra and her friends skipped school to march in the peaceful procession through downtown Los Angeles. For them, American-born citizens, the worst that could happen would be a night in jail. For many of the immigrant workers in the march—their uncles, aunts, parents and neighbors—speaking up for basic recognition and fair treatment could have been the last act of their lives in America.

As Sandra tells this story, you can still glimpse the scared and perplexed thirteen-year-old she once was. She describes her yearning for her eighteenth birthday, the day she could apply for family-based green cards for her own parents. She cannot speak without emotion about the day those green cards arrived two years later. Sandra no longer lives with that radical vulnerability, knowing her parents could disappear to a country she has never visited. Or maybe, since all of us live with the vulnerabilities of our teenage years long after those years are gone, she lives with that vulnerability every day.

Every one of us is a neighbor to communities in suffering. This can literally be true—the pleasant town where I live borders a postindustrial city with one of the highest murder rates in my state. Nearly every reader of this book will live within an hour's drive of a place similarly entrenched in vulnerability without authority—and we all live a short plane flight away from even more extreme examples. Within our businesses and our workplaces, our hospitals and our colleges, in even the healthiest places, there are pockets of persistent and seemingly intractable poverty, material and spiritual.

You might object. Not all workplaces, you might say. What about those darlings of the media, the social media startups of the last decade where every employee is a millionaire, the companies with stratospheric valuations, onsite masseurs and free vegan cuisine in the cafeteria, the firms full of authority and healthy risk-taking?

But in fact these firms also are neighbors to and intertwined with an economic ecosystem that leaves whole communities in suffering. In October 2014 *Wired* magazine reported on the dirty work every social media company must somehow handle: moderating the deluge of exploitative, degrading content posted in unimaginable quantities around the world and around the clock by boors (and increasingly by bots). This is not simply material that might offend those of gentle or puritanical sensibilities, but truly unthinkable representations of real and fictional violence, abuse of women and men, children and animals, and countless other horrors conjured up by the human mind.

Someone has to prevent the average user from encountering these horrors or else all of our news feeds would be regularly infiltrated by retch-inducing images and text. But this means that a human being has to review every degrading image. And that someone is usually a resident of a distant country, employed by an outsourcing firm—at the time of *Wired's* article, largely in the Philippines, thanks to its cheap labor supply and reasonably close ties to Western culture. Philippine young adults do this work because there is no better work to do, and they do it until they are utterly undone by it.

This is the reality of the globalized Internet world, in which the depredations of a few, the pornographers and exploiters who seek power without vulnerability (Exploiting), are foisted on those with no alternative (Suffering) in order to allow the privileged to live in ignorant comfort (Withdrawing). It's a world in which poverty of spirit is bought at near-poverty wages. The flourishing of a few powerful companies—and we who use their services— is a mirage made possible only if you avert your eyes from the vulnerability they outsource to others.

BUILDING AUTHORITY

The existence and persistence of the quadrant called Suffering is the real test of power—a test that all of us with power have failed. The consequences of our failure to fully bear the divine image fall most heavily on those who live in this quadrant with no prospect of escape—the individuals and communities who exist in a state of continual vulnerability.

Making things worse, some well-meaning attempts to intervene in situations of suffering can actually increase vulnerability and undermine authority. As Gary Haugen and Victor Boutros point out in their compelling book *The Locust Effect,* half a century's worth of financial investment in the materially poor world has had surprisingly little effect. Introducing material resources alone into a system of exploitation—treating the symptoms of Suffering without addressing the disease of Exploiting and Withdrawing—actually can increase the vulnerability of the poor. Even at the smallest scale, a family given a few farm animals by a well-intentioned development program can begin to attract the hungry gaze of people willing to do them violence. At the largest scale, global development funds in the hundreds of millions of dollars become powerful incentives to corruption at the highest levels of government.

Too often, our efforts to intervene in suffering end up only reinforcing poverty. It is almost never enough to reduce vulnerability—even though that is what most of us seek to do in our own lives. We must also restore proper authority to individual persons and to whole communities. There is nothing wrong with reducing meaningless risk in people's lives—their vulnerability to hunger or disease. But the best interventions in situations of persistent poverty increase authority as well.

How do we move people stuck in the quadrant called Suffering toward the authority for which they were made? The only truly sustainable response is *to help build lasting authority*. In 2007 I had the opportunity to visit a district in India where bonded labor—modern-day child slavery— had been endemic. But with the help of the Christian humanitarian organization World Vision, these small, materially poor communities had begun to see extraordinary change. A few of World Vision's interventions in that situation were focused on pressing, immediate relief of vulnerability (programs to provide basic food, clean water and shelter), but most were aimed at increasing meaningful authority: savings programs for women (financial savings, especially in communities of great poverty, are an important source of capacity for meaningful action), training and support for local law enforcement (encouraging the kind of legitimate authority that could restrain exploitative moneylenders), and, most memorably for me, the "children's *panchayat*," a village council just for children, where they could practice the responsibility for the community that would be theirs when they came of age.

What I found in that community is what can be found in so many communities marked by suffering: when the gospel begins to transform individuals and communities, it does not simply relieve the most immediate needs. Indeed, many of those needs may remain unmet in any material sense. And yet the gospel restores hope and dignity, meaningful action and meaningful risk. At a distance, you might suppose that systemic injustice and multigenerational vulnerability would leave nothing but misery in their wake. But draw closer to even the greatest suffering and you find people of extraordinary resilience and spiritual power. One of them, for me, is named Isabel.

A PATH APPEARS

Every session of the weekend conference on faith and work, held at an energetic and growing church in Santa Barbara, California, was to begin with an interview between Kyle, the pastor hosting the event, and a member of the congregation talking about their work. The very first story we heard is what I will always remember about that weekend.

Isabel, poised and impeccably dressed, joined Kyle on the stage. She gave a brief summary of her story in proficient, Spanish-inflected English—born in the city of Viña del Mar in Chile, trained and credentialed there as a family counselor. A few years before she had immigrated to the United States with her American husband, awaiting the birth of their son. They settled in Santa Barbara to be near family members. But Isabel discovered that her professional credentials from Chile were not recognized in the United States, and her husband struggled to find steady work. Still, Isabel said gratefully, she had eventually been able to find full-time work.

"And what is that work?" prompted Kyle.

"I clean houses," Isabel said. The Santa Barbara hills are full of spacious homes, and nearly every one employs a Hispanic woman as a cleaner. That was the work that Isabel had found—and could speak about in theological terms.

"How do you see your work reflecting God's work?" Kyle asked.

"If you look in the book of Genesis, in the beginning, the world is in darkness," Isabel said. "There is no order. God is a God of order—he orders every single life, changes every life from darkness to light in Jesus. And that is my motivation as I work. Everything I do is from God, not from man. Jesus washed the feet of his disciples, and we are to do the same: be a servant with love. If I am cleaning a toilet—well, that is something that needs to be done to order the world and to wash the feet of others. There is no sadness about that; it's a joy. The greatest example of servanthood in my life is the Holy Spirit, because he guides me. I listen to his voice, and I say, 'Yes, sir.'"

Just to make sure you understand the significance of this

near-verbatim transcript from her interview: in a few sentences, Isabel had just given us a trinitarian vision of the work of house cleaning.

> In a few sentences, Isabel had just given us a trinitarian vision of the work of house cleaning.

"Do you encounter brokenness in the work you do?" Kyle asked.

"Of course," Isabel replied. "It's sad to see people who have everything beautiful, everything perfect. They contract with you so their world can continue perfect and clean. But you realize their life is empty. So I have to be light for them. Every single home I go to, I pray for that family, that they can find him. If he will use me, amen. If not, amen—he will send somebody else."

When Isabel is not working or caring for her own family, she is volunteering with a center called Immigrant Hope that serves other women from Latin America, most of whom also clean houses. Isabel teaches courses that help them prepare for drivers license exams and the tests required for citizenship in the United States. "The Lord Jesus is teaching me that we are all immigrants," she told me, "and our real home is with him. So we should be showing others his love and mercy, and how much he loves those whose lives are broken. By addressing very practical needs, we show them the one who makes everything new."

I called Isabel to ask her permission to quote from that interview in this book. She asked for time to pray about it, then asked if we could speak by phone a few days later. It turned out that Isabel had not primarily been praying about whether she should give permission for her story to be in this book—God had apparently settled that question quickly, and it was fine. Instead, she had been praying for me, by name, and God had given her specific words to speak to me, specific instructions for my own prayer life and a set of verses from the New Testament letter 1 Peter to guide me. Printed on a piece of paper, they sit on my desk as I write.

Isabel has authority, something you discover the moment you meet her. She speaks and acts meaningfully in everything she does. Her authority does not come primarily from her circumstances—those reflect the vulnerability of the countless immigrants who, their deeper gifts so often unrecognized and unused, serve in jobs that few Americans will take at all, let alone take gladly. There is much in Isabel's life and story, both spoken and left unsaid between the lines of her testimony, that speaks of the vulnerability without authority that comes to so many in a broken world.

But her story has been transformed by another story— her life's action has been made meaningful by being caught up in the story of the gospel. She has moved from quadrant II to quadrant I, from Suffering to Flourishing—and she is bringing others with her.

This can be true for us as well. No one escapes this quadrant of human experience. As we will see in the final chapters of this book, we actually will be called to seek out suffering, to go to its depths, if we truly want to bring flourishing to the world. But when we journey to the heart of suffering, whether by circumstance or by choice, we are only going where Another has gone before us. When we find our place in that story and in that journey, our vulnerability, too, becomes the path to flourishing.

4

WITHDRAWING

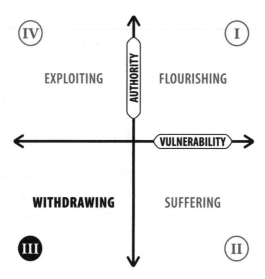

As a father, I discovered what exactly the Gospel of Luke had meant by "swaddling clothes." My newborn son loved nothing so much as to be tightly wrapped in a blanket, arms and legs neatly tucked into a package, and held. Unswaddled, he would fuss and squirm; properly swaddled, he became both calm and alert, able to take in the world around him without anxiety. The swaddling clothes bound him but also comforted him. It is worth pondering that the Savior of the world, too, was swaddled in his own infancy—protected from both action and risk.

Within a few weeks, of course, my son outgrew his swaddling blankets and his desire for them. (And not all babies take to swaddling, as his sister made fiercely clear when she came along a few years later.) But for the first years of his life, it was my deepest desire as a parent to protect him from too much of either authority or vulnerability. We moved tantalizing but fragile objects out of his reach; we swooped in to pick him up when he wandered too far on the sidewalk or the playground; we scanned every room for sources of risk. A healthy childhood is one where both capacity for action and exposure to meaningful risk are meted out in measured doses, gradually increasing as the child matures.

So if Suffering is the quadrant none of us have been able to avoid, the quadrant of Withdrawing is where we all began—and at the beginning it was called Safety.

No authority and no vulnerability—or at least no awareness of either one. Unborn, we had no capacity for meaningful action, and we were blissfully unconscious of meaningful risk. We had not yet discovered the world with its history, future, possibilities and dangers. Just as well, because we were unformed and unready for them. If we had been too exposed to either authority or vulnerability at that most tender stage of human life, we would not be alive today.

Such safety is a fleeting thing. Far too many childhoods are compromised by the early introduction of too much vulnerability and too much authority. This very day there are children picking through smoldering heaps of garbage in the ports of Africa and Asia where our discarded electronics go for recycling, making tiny sums of money to support their families while exposing their lungs to toxic fumes and their hands and feet to jagged metal and glass. Others are being handed lethal weapons and trained in killing before they have developed the moral compunctions of adulthood; still others are exposed to the degraded passions of desperate men. Few parents would wish this kind of crash course in the cruelty of the world on their children, but many parents themselves live deep in the quadrant called Suffering. There is no vulnerability deeper, no lack of authority more crushing, than the inability to protect your own child from harm. Millions of parents on this planet know that reality all too well.

One night as I tucked my daughter into her bed, safe beneath her down comforter and properly lavished with kisses and hugs, and prayed for her safety, I unexpectedly sensed the unmistakable voice of Another addressing me in return. "I hear your prayers," this voice seemed to say kindly but sternly. "But I also hear the prayers every night of parents who can offer their children no protection." It was not a rebuke; it was an invitation to understand exactly how much anguish is brought before "the Father from whom all fatherhood takes its name." And perhaps it was a reminder that there is another way to fail your children: too much swaddling.

THE ONLY THING MONEY CAN BUY

For almost all of human history, parents' nightly prayers for their children's protection were offered in the face of urgent and unavoidable vulnerability. Only in these last decades, in privileged corners of the world, has any child been tucked into bed with such utter security as my own children have known. Perhaps parents have always been tempted to swaddle their children for too long, protecting them from as much of the world as they can—but only recently have we been able to actually succeed.

We have a saying in our family: *The only thing money can buy is bubble wrap.* Affluence cannot ultimately remove the vulnerability that is our human condition and our true human calling, but it can swaddle you in so many layers of insulation that you will never

The only thing money can buy is bubble wrap.

be able to fully feel it—or to freely move. It can keep you swaddled far beyond your tender years, well into an adulthood of risk-averse entitlement.

If you settle down in this corner, even your ambitions will become carefully circumscribed, following well-marked paths to good compensation and social respectability. The slippery pole of ascent to an Ivy League education may be fiercely contested—a friend who works in college admissions jokes that "helicopter parents" have now been replaced by "bulldozer parents," who clear every obstacle from their children's paths, and "drone parents," who hover invisibly overhead and then swoop in with overwhelming force when their progeny is endangered. But the competition is so fierce precisely because the prize is so predictable: a golden ticket to career paths that are carefully staked out in advance to maximize reward and minimize risk. If you look at life this way, there is nowhere so safe as Harvard Yard. If you aim for real flourishing, there is nowhere more dangerous.

The greatest challenge of success is the freedom it gives you to opt out of real risk and real authority. Entrepreneurs who take on substantial authority in the face of real risk, and have the fortune to be rewarded for that venture into the quadrant called Flourishing, can cash out of the game, turning the fruits of their success into so much stored wealth that they can retreat from risk—and authority—

altogether. The more that you know, or sense, that your success was as much a product of luck and timing as of skill and character, the less likely you will be to ever dare to risk that much again.

The Eternal Cruise

We have to begin in Safety in order to flourish, but to cling to it in adulthood is folly. When I think about this quadrant, and the strange allure it holds for us later in life, I think about one of the leisure fantasies of the modern world: taking a cruise. Not a *crossing,* mind you, the epic journey from the Old World to the New across the Atlantic that some of my ancestors undertook, a one-way trip with a destination and something different and difficult waiting at the other end. And not even the kind of cruises, like those up into the glacier bays of Alaska or the fjords of Norway, that allow you to come close to natural wonders impossible to apprehend any other way—the kind that leave you feeling awed, humbled, properly small and full of praise. I'm thinking of the cruises without destinations that circle around the tourist-friendly ports of tropical islands, cruises where the real desire and delight is to be on the ship itself.

> We have to begin in Safety in order to flourish, but to cling to it in adulthood is folly.

As you can guess, I am firmly in the non-cruising part of humanity—the part that chortles at David Foster Wallace's epic essay about such a cruise, "A Supposedly Fun Thing I'll Never Do Again," and hopes never to do it in the first place. But I can appreciate why my cruising acquaintances think that a cruise, with its languid days and nights, its bountiful buffets, its complete disengagement from terrestrial life, is a marvelous vacation. After all, a cruise is about as pure a return to the quadrant III of childhood as you could ask for. Food is abundant, demands on your time are minimal, the sun is bright. You have absolutely no authority—even if the captain invites you to visit the bridge, you will be forcibly restrained if you attempt to take command of the ship—and, for all practical purposes, no vulnerability either. (We will set aside the handful of cruises from hell where the engines give out, the ship starts turning in slow wide gyres in the Gulf of Mexico and the passengers spell out "HELP" with their bodies on the Lido deck—as well as the surprisingly frequent cruises where some virus colonizes the kitchen and half the crew and passengers become ill, or those where the steady rolling of the ship leaves you bedridden for days. As you can see, I'm just not that much of a fan of cruises.)

This is all fine—as vacation. It is delicious for a few days or perhaps even a week.

But what if your whole life were a cruise? Year after year of others deciding where you will go, what's for dinner, anticipating your needs and protecting you from any real harm? That would be less than human. Indeed, it would be something quite like hell. The magnificent Pixar film *WALL-E* depicts exactly such a cruise gone wrong, set in a not-so-distant future in which all of humanity has fled the mess their own greed created. The first passengers are told it will be a brief excursion, but instead it goes on for centuries with no hope of return, and each generation becomes less capable and more dependent on the robots who take over their image-bearing calling.

Like all Pixar films, *WALL-E* is about what it is to be fully human. With his insatiable curiosity, his delight in both order and abundance, and his willingness to fall in love with a lovely and lethal robot far more advanced than himself, the little trash-collecting robot is the truly flourishing character in the midst of Earth's garbage and the spaceliner *Axiom*'s decadence.

But for all of WALL-E's charm, he turns out to be a supporting character. Once we meet the ship's captain, who has been reduced to pudgy inactivity deep in the corner of Safety and Withdrawing, the real conflict unfolds. The captain represents all of us human beings in all of our infantilized incapacity. His awakening to the delights of an almost-forgotten Earth and the call of stewardship—and his decision to wrest command of the ship from autopilot—is the laugh-and-shout-out-loud climax of the movie (hilariously accompanied by the strains of *Also sprach Zarathustra*). We cheer for the captain because he is claiming his authority and embracing meaningful risk—exiting Withdrawing in hopes of a return to Flourishing.

We are not meant to be eternal cruise-ship passengers. We are meant for more than leisure. This is true for our own sakes, but it is also true because, like the diminished human beings aboard the *Axiom*, we are still responsible for a world gone wrong. The deepest reason for the call out of Withdrawing is not our own health, though this quadrant is none too healthy or satisfying a place to live. It is far more about the neighbors and the created order we have neglected, who have no option to board a cruise away from vulnerability, who live, in some cases quite literally, among the trash our affluence has discarded. To disengage from the profound needs of those caught in suffering is to reject the call to bear the image of God. We all began in the protection of paradise, but attempting to make that safety our final state will in fact consign us to hell.

> We are not meant to be eternal cruise-ship passengers. We are meant for more than leisure.

SIMULATED AUTHORITY

There is, however, a subtler version of withdrawing than the pure vacancy of a cruise. Most of us would in fact find ourselves bored to tears after a few weeks of perpetual vacation—our thirst for flourishing is too strong to completely abandon the call to authority and vulnerability. But the technological culture has another, stronger trick up its sleeve—not total disengagement, but powerful and rewarding *simulations* of engagement. The real temptation for most of us is not complete apathy but activities that simulate meaningful action and meaningful risk without actually asking much of us or transforming much in us.

So if you really want to see what withdrawing looks like in affluent, technological America, you don't have to visit a port of call. You just have to turn on the PlayStation in your living room.

Just like cruises and other forms of vacation, games have an important place in a healthy life. For children, games are a primary way of practicing the authority and vulnerability that will be their calling in adult life. For adults, games' simplicity and rule-based rewards are a welcome break from the open-ended, complicated demands of maturity.

> If you really want to see what withdrawing looks like in affluent, technological America, you just have to turn on the PlayStation in your living room.

But just as a cruise starts to degrade from heaven to hell if it becomes your daily life, games, especially technologically enhanced ones, are a dangerous place to live. Very few of us can afford a perpetual cruise. But we can afford video games—they are priced at the sweet spot of consumer discretionary demand. We would have to rearrange our whole lives to spend our remaining years on cruises. Video games, however, gladly take up residence at the center of our homes. Most of us would start to get fidgety after a few days onboard a ship. Video games are a far more satisfying version of withdrawing—because while you are engrossed in them, you feel totally convinced that you are flourishing.

Games confer authority. But video games (and most screen-based forms of recreation) confer authority more quickly and more completely than any real-world game does. To become the quarterback for the pickup game in my neighbor's backyard would require me to demonstrate some level of mastery of the game of football to other human beings. Even being a backyard quarterback is probably beyond the reach of my puny arms, but to become a quarterback in the NFL requires nearly superhuman abilities and discipline.

To become an "NFL quarterback" in the video game *Madden Football,* however, requires little more than choosing an avatar and pressing a button. Suddenly you are vested with all of the authority, and much of the ability, of your chosen celebrity player. Of course there is a learning curve in *Madden Football*—if there were not, it would quickly become repetitive and boring. Your onscreen self will drop passes, get sacked and make poor decisions. But with a little dedication, almost anyone can become a capable *Madden Football* quarterback. The learning curve is far shallower in the video game than in the real game—if it were not, almost no one would find it rewarding to play.

The game also gives you an experience of vulnerability—exposure to meaningful risk—but even more than the ersatz authority you gain with technology's help, this vulnerability is well and truly a mirage. Play enough *Madden Football* and you really will acquire certain kinds of skills, thin though they may be—that is, you will gain some real authority in understanding and playing the game of football. But no matter how much you play, you will never get a concussion, you will never be cut from the team, and you will lose nothing of value in the "real world" outside the game (except, of course, whatever real capacities you could have developed in the time you spent becoming an expert at *Madden Football*). The authority may be largely simulated, but the vulnerability is entirely an illusion.

This is the power of video games—the reason they are far more absorbing than TV, with its one-way, passive consumption, and a bigger industry than movies after just a few decades in existence ($93 billion worldwide in 2013 compared to the movie industry's $88 billion). They give us accessible simulations of flourishing life, the life which we all crave—the life of action and risk, the life of adventure and conquest, even (in some games) the life of romance and the satisfactions of community.

But they are only simulations. There is a marked asymmetry between the skill you acquire in the world of space, time and flesh-and-blood bodies, and the skill you acquire in the virtual world of screens and controllers. Skill from the real world translates well, generally, into the virtual world. If you are skilled at the actual embodied game of (American) football, you will likely be good at the video game *Madden Football*. If you are an accomplished race-car driver, you can probably quickly master *Forza Motorsport 5*. But the skills do not transfer, or transfer only minimally, in the other direction. Being good at *Madden Football* will have very little effect in your neighbor's backyard, let alone on the turf at Soldier Field.

Ironically, the reason video games develop so little real skill is that they are *too* rewarding. Real authority is a tedious business. Developing the depth of competence required to play an instrument, pilot an aircraft or transplant a human organ requires thousands of hours of

> Ironically, the reason video games develop so little real skill is that they are *too* rewarding.

unstimulating, unstinting practice that gives us little immediate sense of authority.

And yet this kind of patient development, which is itself a form of vulnerability, is the only path to real authority. In video games, every warrior has qualified for the Special Forces; every basketball player has a 30-inch vertical leap. Not to mention that wielding lethal violence leaves no emotional scars, just a pleasant sense of victory—and the bodies on the screen stay perpetually young and vital. The more you give yourself over to simulations, the more true authority and true vulnerability recede from your life. Video games give us a shortcut to the godlike figures we wish ourselves to be but are too inconstant to actually become.

FRICTION-FREE ACTIVISM

If this simulated flourishing were restricted to the world of leisure—cruises and games—at least we would know that it was not the real world. But the reward structure of video games—the simulated authority and vulnerability of virtual reality—is increasingly colonizing our interactions with the most serious matters of the real world as well. Like technologically mediated entertainment, the technology of social media is becoming more "gamified" by the year as developers learn how to tap into the deep human hunger for simulations of authority and vulnerability. In social media, you can engage in nearly friction-free experiences of activism, expressing enthusiasm, solidarity or outrage (all powerful sensations of authority) for your chosen cause with the click of a few buttons.

Like all media (including books like this one!), social media are largely what we make of them—escapist or transforming depending on what we expect from them and how we use them. In far-flung places in the world, an emerging generation has used media like Twitter to coordinate impressive examples of meaningful action combined with extraordinary risk—the 2014 protests in Hong Kong and the outcry in the United States about police practices and race being recent examples as I write this book.

But these two uses of social media have two key features in common. First, they were largely used by people living deep in Suffering—exposed to meaningful risk without being granted meaningful capacity for action by their societies. Second, they led to embodied, in-the-flesh experiences of action in community. When media are tools that help those who have lacked the capacity for action take action, and bring them together to bear risk together rather than be paralyzed in Suffering, they can lead to real change.

But when the residents of the comfortable affluence of Withdrawing use media to *simulate* engagement, to give ourselves a sense of making a personal investment when in fact our activity risks nothing and forms nothing new in

our characters, then "virtual activism" is in fact a way of
doubling down on withdrawing, holding on to one's invulnerability and incapacity while creating a sensation of in-
volvement. Only when technology serves a genuine, embodied, risky move toward flourishing is it something other
than an opiate for the mass elite—the drug that leaves us
mired in our apathy and our neighbors in their need.

The Safety Generation

Before the current era, almost no one could stay in Withdrawing beyond the early years of childhood. The world
was too harsh and human cultures too demanding of real
maturity. Society could not afford to tolerate those who
shirked the authority and vulnerability that were necessary
to eke out flourishing from the world. Consider the eight-
year-old child sent to the barn to milk a cow. She has already been granted real flourishing—the authority of dominion over a creature, responsible for its flourishing and
benefiting from its abundance, along with the vulnerability
of being a small human being next to a massive bovine. It
is a kind of flourishing that a child milking a cow in *Minecraft* (accomplished, I'm told, by right clicking while
"holding" a bucket) will never know.

But today we have to constantly choose to move up and
to the right. If there is one temptation that seems to me
endemic to the emerging generation of young adults, it is

to choose Withdrawing—to retreat from authority and vulnerability alike. At a worship service one evening in the spring of 2014, I presented these four quadrants—especially the three where all of us spend far too much of our lives—to several hundred college students. We invited students to come forward for prayer, to be liberated for the abundant and flourishing life we were made for. We were astonished and moved as more than one hundred students came forward for personal prayer. It was one of the manifestations of the power and presence of God that you cannot orchestrate but can only receive, and we stayed long into the night praying alongside these friends.

The next day, the college chaplain and the team of counselors who had offered prayer gathered to debrief the previous night's event. I was curious about which quadrant most of the prayer requests had come from. Were students wrestling with experiences of persistent vulnerability without authority? Or the temptation to grasp authority without vulnerability? Or the retreat from both? Overwhelmingly, every prayer leader reported, it was Withdrawing. The domain of inaction, of fear of exposure, of safety. One young man approached me for prayer and confided that in each of his four closest friendships, he was experiencing overwhelming temptation to minimize risk, avoid real engagement and abandon them.

Amidst safety the world has never before known, the

greatest spiritual struggle many of us face is to be willing to take off our bubble wrap.

THE PATH FROM WITHDRAWING

The good news about escaping the Withdrawing quadrant is that pretty much any move, toward either authority or vulnerability, is a step in the right direction. Perhaps the two best beginning moves, for those of us swaddled in affluence and intoxicated by our technology, are into the natural world—the world of stars, snow and rain, trees and deserts—and into the relational world—the world of real bodies with heartbeats, hands and faces.

Turn off your devices and go for a walk or a run, not just on days when the weather is pleasant but on days when the wind is fierce, the rain is falling or the humidity is high. Shiver or sweat, feel fatigue in your limbs, hear the sounds of the city or the countryside unfiltered by headphones. Choose to go to places—the ocean, the mountains, or a broad, wide field—where you will feel small rather than grand.

> Choose to go to places— the ocean, the mountains, or a broad, wide field— where you will feel small rather than grand.

Dare to walk across campus or across town without looking at a screen.

Decide to introduce yourself to one new person each day—just to learn their name and give them yours, with no further agenda.

Brew coffee or tea, sit with a friend and ask them questions—questions just one step riskier than the last time you talked. As you listen, observe the flickers of sadness or hope that cross their face. Try to imagine what it must be like to live their story, suffer their losses, dream their dreams. Pray with them and dare to put into words their heart's desires, and dare to ask God to grant them.

The next time you travel, decide not to be a tourist, who uses material wealth to purchase experiences of vicarious significance—being in places that make us feel grand and worth noticing. Instead, travel like a pilgrim, who travels to encounter people who have been sanctified by suffering. Seek out people who live on the cruel edges of the world. Accompany them in person, at least for short seasons, in their authority and vulnerability. Share what you have with them in sufficient measure that your generosity feels vulnerable, emptying your bank account to the point that you instinctively start to pray for daily bread.

Our affluence has left us unready for the tragedy and danger of the world. But what we cannot see when we are caught in Withdrawing is that there is something far better ahead, pleasures which we must be made strong enough to bear. We will only discover them if someone unwraps us and calls us forth. And the great glad news of the gospel is that someone has.

EXPLOITING

As I write these words, the world's most apparently successful tyrant is a man named Kim Jong Un.

Along with a small band of elite leaders, Kim rules the Democratic People's Republic of Korea—better known to the rest of the world as North Korea—with absolute authority. Like his father and grandfather, he has ruthlessly eliminated anyone who might pose a threat to his power, including ordering the execution of elder members of his own family. Causing even the most minor disturbance to the leader's authority or his sense of national pride—say, turning in an insufficiently pleasing design for a new airport—is a death warrant for officials high or low.

If we believe the reports of former chefs and, improbably enough, movie directors employed by the Kim family, Kim Jong Un has enjoyed a life of extraordinary privilege and comfort. But in spite of the relentlessly upbeat reports that emerge from the state-controlled news agency, this abundance never spreads beyond a tiny circle. Most of Kim's subjects live in profound poverty, and every one of his country's citizens lives with well-justified fear.

Kim Jong Un lives up and to the left, in quadrant IV, Exploiting. But the people he leads live deep in quadrant II. Tyranny and suffering, exploiting and poverty, always are found together. Indeed, you know you are encountering a situation of injustice when a few people in a system enjoy authority without vulnerability at the price of most people in that system suffering vulnerability without authority.

Tyrants and dictators live at the most extreme edge of exploitation, with their people living at the most extreme edge of suffering. But Exploiting is found anywhere people seek to maximize power while eliminating risk.

And it turns out to be the most seductive and dangerous quadrant of all.

RISK AND REWARD

We human beings, as one ingeniously devised experiment after another has demonstrated, are considerably more motivated by the fear of loss than the possibility of gain. If I give you fifty dollars, then give you the choice of simply walking away with that fifty dollars or wagering it in a bet where you have a chance of making five hundred dollars, you are far more likely to choose the safe fifty than take the bet. Just a few moments ago, you had nothing—but once we have something, we want to keep it.

This tendency toward "loss aversion" is not universal—some of us will take on much more risk than others—but overall it is consistent and powerful enough to affect whole industries, economies and nations. The completely rational actor of economics, that fictional creature sometimes called *homo economicus,* would balance risk against reward in strictly mathematical fashion—but we *homo sapiens* weigh risk and reward using very different scales.

And this explains something interesting about our 2x2 grid. Flourishing, I've been arguing, requires both authority *and* vulnerability in equal measure. The true life for which we were made will require us both to act and to risk. But we do not pursue these two good things with the same wholeheartedness—or even the same halfheartedness. Most of us are far more willing to move up than we are to move to the right—indeed, we are more likely to spend significant amounts of energy moving *away* from the right than *toward* the right at all.

It's loss aversion in action. Authority corresponds to the ability to add something to the world—the possibility of gain. Vulnerability corresponds to the possibility—though only the possibility—of loss. In our daily choices, both conscious and unconscious, the possibility of loss counts far more than the possibility of gain. That is why so many of us end up moving to the left, away from vulnerability.

That is why, to many of us, authority without risk sounds like a much better deal. Perhaps the only real difference between us and Kim Jong Un is that for him, by an accident of birth, that dream of living up and to the left came terribly true.

YOUR BRAIN ON DRUGS

Take a social situation every human being has to deal with at some point: walking into a room full of people we do not know. For most of us, that is a meaningful risk. (For a few ultra-extroverts, it's sheer delight—a hundred friends you haven't met yet! You know who you are. The rest of us know who you are, too, and we both envy you and think you are truly bizarre.) After the first blissful days of our earliest childhood, we learned, usually the hard way, that there is vulnerability in crowds.

Think about the vulnerability of the first days and months of your adult life, your first season away from home, perhaps on a university campus, and the simultaneous excitement and trepidation of your first big on-campus party—full of seemingly happy, confident, attractive peers.

What if I could hand something to the eighteen-year-old version of you walking into that party—something you could hold in your hand, something that would increase your authority and decrease your vulnerability? Something that as you held it—and sipped it—gradually eased your discomfort and enhanced your excitement? It wouldn't be strictly legal, in the United States at least—but it would be very appealing indeed.

At the moment that you begin to use alcohol to manage your vulnerability in a social situation, you are heading up and to the left. At first, and up to a point, it will work wonders. A few drinks will take the edge off the sense of risk and exposure you felt when you walked in. They will give you a heightened sense of power and possibility. You will be living the intoxicating life of a minor god.

But over time, as with all addictions (and all idols), the effect begins to wear off. A higher and higher dose is needed for the same effect. And gradually, the thing that once delivered authority without vulnerability begins to expose you to risk and rob you of authority. In the long run, unless you are delivered by a miracle of grace, you will find that the very thing that promised authority without vulnerability has betrayed you, handing you over to the depths of suffering—vulnerability without authority.

Our daily lives are filled with these small choices—small at first, but over time, becoming a deep dependence on strategies that preserve our sense of action while minimizing our sense of risk. The church once enumerated seven deadly sins—lust, gluttony, greed, sloth, wrath, envy and pride. Most of them are ways of pursuing authority without vulnerability. Sex without commitment (lust), food without moderation (gluttony), goods without limit (greed), anger without compassion (wrath), and above all the pursuit of autonomous, godlike power (pride)—all these are forms of what Scripture calls, most comprehensively, idolatry, the use of created things to pursue godlike power without risk or limit. (Sloth, of course, is the deadly sin that corresponds to Withdrawing, the safety of risking nothing in the world; and envy may be the besetting sin of Suffering, the jealousy and bitterness of those who can see only their own vulnerability and others' authority.) All these are just variations on the promises that accompanied the very first idol, the fruit proffered by the serpent in the Garden: "You will be like God"—unlimited authority—

and, "You will not die"—none of that vulnerable creaturely dependence.

Perhaps the most characteristic idol of our time is online pornography because it fuses two of the most powerful idols of our time: sex and technology. Available at a click are vicarious experiences of sexual knowledge and conquest— authority that begins with the ability to see others in naked and vulnerable states, and escalates, in "harder" forms of porn, to more extravagant and ultimately demonic forms of domination. But these experiences of godlike knowledge and control are almost always consumed from a position of complete invulnerability, in isolation and secrecy.

The irony is stunning: the twentieth-century sexual revolution's promise of "freedom" has given way to a twenty-first-century epidemic of attenuated, mediated sexual escapism. Even most secular observers now admit that pornography undermines the capacity of men and women to maintain healthy levels of sexual desire for their actual partners, let alone experience the true authority and vulnerability of embodied encounter. Who could have predicted such an outcome? Anyone could have predicted it—anyone who understood the power of idols to promise freedom and deliver slavery, to offer authority and deliver vulnerability, to whisper fantasies of power but end up with us completely in their grip.

While some of us, by the sheer grace of God, manage to

escape the lure of the most powerful idols, not one of us does not have some habit, some recurring pattern of thought, substance or device that we turn to when we are feeling vulnerable—something that assuages our vulnerability and elevates our sense of capacity to act. They offer us, in a word, *control*—for the very essence of control is authority without vulnerability, the ability to act without the possibility of loss. Control is the dream of the risk- and loss-averse, the promise of every idol and the quest of every person who has tasted vulnerability and vowed never to be exposed in that way again.

But control is an illusion. In fact, all of the quadrant called Exploiting is an illusion. There is, in the long run, no such thing as true authority without true vulnerability. Our idols inevitably fail us, generally sooner rather than later. And as they begin to fail, we begin to grasp ever more violently for the control we thought they promised and we deserved. This is why the end result of life in this quadrant is exploitation—ripping from the world, and especially from those too weak to resist, the good things our idols promised but are failing to deliver.

> Control is the dream of the risk- and loss-averse, the promise of every idol.

As a few people pursue and even for a season grasp the idol of control and exploitation, the community around them falls into the poverty that exploitation always brings.

PHIL AND LESLIE

My friends Phil and Leslie are driving home one night after
a full day of work as campus ministers at the University of
California, Berkeley. They stop for a few groceries, turn the
corner onto the avenue where they live, and see the flashing
blue and red lights of a police car behind them. *Do we have
a taillight out?* Phil wonders.

Within minutes, six police cars have appeared, lights
flashing and sirens wailing. Later Phil would write about
what happened:

> A voice from a loudspeaker told me to roll down my
> window. The voice told me to open my car door,
> keeping my hands visible at all times. *Take four steps
> away from the car, keeping your hands clearly visible,*
> I was told. The instructions went on: *Face the car.
> Bend down on both knees. Put your hands on the
> ground. Lie face down. Turn your face to the right.*

Lying on the ground, Phil is handcuffed and placed in
one police car. Leslie is subjected to the same procedure.
Now they are in separate police cars, watching as police
search their vehicle (turning up groceries and Bible study
materials, and nothing more). Someone has been robbed
at gunpoint a couple of blocks away, an officer tells Phil,
and he and Leslie "match the description" of the robbers.
The officer ignores Phil's offer to produce the time-stamped
receipt from the grocery store that could clear them of

suspicion. Instead, Phil is removed from the police car, still handcuffed, so the victim can attempt to identify him. His neighbors watch from their porches as he stands in the glare of headlights and flashlights.

Half an hour later, with a brusque, "Sorry for the inconvenience," and a pointed reminder that they have not been cleared from suspicion, the handcuffs are removed and they are allowed to leave.

There is something you'd never guess that makes this story ironic, and something you should be able to easily guess that makes it all too common and tragic.

What you'd never guess is that Phil's father-in-law—Leslie's father—is the chief of police in a city just a few miles away from where they were detained. She grew up knowing the great dignity of police work, along with its dangers and demands, and seeing her father honored for his courageous and faithful leadership.

What you probably could guess is that Phil and Leslie are black.

THE MILITARY AND THE POLICE

One vulnerability every community faces is crime. Some crime emerges from the frustration of the quadrant called Exploiting, the failure of idols to deliver, the indulgence of the deadly sins of lust, greed and the rest, and the exploitation that follows. Some crime may come from the deprivation of

Suffering, a desperate bid to obtain some means of authority in the world. But because crime depends on secrecy and violence, it can never offer the real flourishing that its perpetrators seek. Crime leaves the whole community, including its perpetrators, wounded and further from flourishing.

So every human community has to find a way to limit, prevent and punish crime. But the approaches we take to crime say a great deal about which quadrant governs our imaginations. What Phil and Leslie encountered that night, and what so many African Americans encounter routinely in their interactions with the police, is a form of policing that seeks greater and greater authority with less and less vulnerability—which leads, as all attempts to move into this quadrant do, to others experiencing what Phil and Leslie did that night, the suffering of vulnerability without authority.

Police work is inherently high in meaningful risk, especially in a country like the United States, which has as many guns as citizens. The police officers (not all of whom were white) who stopped Phil and Leslie were in a potentially vulnerable situation themselves, knowing that there were armed robbers somewhere in their precinct. Few other professions call their members to expose themselves to danger in the way that police must routinely do. It is entirely reasonable, and good for everyone's flourishing, that we seek to manage the risks that police face on our behalf.

But in recent years many American police forces, encouraged by lavish federal grants, have added weapons and tactics previously only used by military units. Military weaponry and armor aim to vastly reduce vulnerability while vastly increasing authority. A man in body armor in a military-style tank has more capacity for action, and less vulnerability, than the traditional police officer patrolling on foot or even in a vehicle, armed only with a baton and pistol. And while everything the police did during their stop of Phil and Leslie may have been legal, it is not hard to see that it was all designed to create a situation where the police were in complete control.

Control is a valid military objective. Indeed, the ultimate goal of military action is *conquest*—all authority for the victor, no remaining capacity for meaningful action for the loser (to "surrender" is to be incapable of meaningful action). The goal of military forces is to "control the theater"—to be the only actor with the capacity for meaningful action.

But the goal of a police force can be neither conquest nor control. The goal of police power is flourishing—actually *increasing* the capacity for meaningful action in a community. In a community with effective policing, more people have more authority. Military authority is zero-sum; police authority, properly used, increases the total authority in a community.

The move toward militarized policing is an asymmetrical increase of authority rather than a simultaneous increase of authority and vulnerability. And so it is very likely to be a movement in the direction of Exploiting, not Flourishing. Indeed, some experts on law enforcement argue that effective police patrols were undermined when they began to be conducted by car instead of on foot. Patrols by vehicle are a significant move away from the meaningful risks taken by departments that emphasize what is called "community policing," an approach to law enforcement that emphasizes interaction and relationship between police and the neighborhoods they serve.

And like all attempts to secure authority without vulnerability, the pursuit of quadrant IV-style policing often fails to deliver what it promises. Police forces that distance themselves from their own community find that they are less and less capable of meaningful action and more exposed to risk. Armor protects, but it also restricts. A law enforcement officer in a tank has only a very few options in relating to a crowd, most of them violent—so while he has undoubted firepower, he may actually have less authority than a lone individual standing face to face with the crowd. Over time, any police force that relies on such asymmetric power will find itself losing the authority that really counts, the ability to prevent rather than just punish crime and disorder.

THE VULNERABILITY OF OTHERS

In high school physics we learn (or at least hear about!) the physical laws of conservation—of mass, energy and momentum. The universe is designed in such a way that we cannot actually get rid of or create mass or energy, only move them around.

I am not sure there is a "law of conservation of vulnerability" in the same strict sense, but it is still a general rule: *vulnerability shed by one group of people is inevitably borne by others' suffering.*

Or to put it another way, the pursuit of authority without vulnerability always comes at the price of causing others to live with vulnerability without authority. In fact, the pursuit of authority without vulnerability *multiplies* vulnerability without authority. The resulting suffering is always far greater and longer lasting than whatever momentary benefit came from exploiting.

> Vulnerability shed by one group of people is inevitably borne by others' suffering.

So the criminals who committed an armed robbery in Phil and Leslie's neighborhood, grabbing goods they had not earned from someone vulnerable to their weapons of force, caused an entire community to suffer increased vulnerability. Likewise, though the police may have acted within the law and with the best of intentions, the tactics they used to restrain Phil and Leslie reinforced all kinds of vulnerabilities.

The person addicted to drugs purchases sensations of godlike power and control—but their family suffers neglect, at best, while they are high and exposure to their explosions of anger when the high wears off. The person addicted to pornography pursues sexual authority—or at least a simulation of it, "knowing" others in graphic detail—without sexual vulnerability, without being known. But this experience of sexuality without vulnerability comes at the price of the exploitation of people who are exposed, literally and figuratively, to the porn user without the authority that would be granted them in a genuine relationship of love and intimacy. Often the person made most vulnerable of all is the porn user's spouse, neglected in the quest for a relationship of one-way fantasy and control. Instead of living in mutual authority with vulnerability, the choice by one partner to seek out Exploiting ends up consigning the other to Suffering.

The first things any idol takes from its worshipers are their relationships. Idols know and care nothing for the exchange of authority and vulnerability that happens in the context of love—and the demonic powers that lurk behind them, and lure us to them, despise love. So the

> The first things any idol takes from its worshipers are their relationships.

best early warning sign that you are drifting toward Exploiting—seeking authority without vulnerability in your work, in your entertainment, in alcohol or coffee or chocolate (or whatever may be your drug of choice, in pornography or in romance novels)—is that your closest relationships begin to decay.

It is those relationships, after all, that could grant you the greatest real capacity for meaningful action. But they also demand of you the greatest personal risk. And as you drift up and to the left, those who depend on you for love, friendship and support sink down and to the right. Worst off are those already at great risk—the youngest, the oldest, those who contribute the least to our sensations of power and who expose us to the greatest sense of our own limits. They can only flourish if we resist the temptations of the quadrant called Exploiting—and the more we pursue Exploiting, the more they are swallowed up by Suffering.

In the long run, though, it is not just the most vulnerable who suffer from those who pursue the idolatry of Exploiting. The scathing biblical critique of idols and their makers is that those who make them become like them— dull and ultimately dead. The idol that begins by promising authority without vulnerability inexorably ends up delivering vulnerability without authority. The drink that initially delivers such a sensation of ecstasy and freedom ends up robbing its users of the most basic capacity for action. Tyranny is the most powerful form of government in human affairs—until, one day, suddenly it is the weakest. Rare is the tyrant who goes to his grave secure in his power—let alone having created a system that would allow his heirs to hold on to their power generation after generation. The country of North Korea, in its third generation of tyranny, is the exception that proves the rule. There is almost nothing so certain in international affairs as that the North Korean regime, one way or another, will fail and fall. The only question is whether its collapse will, by God's grace, be merciful and relatively peaceful or involve one last spasm of brutality. The more complete the flight to the upper left corner, the more certain the final judgment.

Indeed, one way to understand the pervasive theme of judgment and hell in the New Testament is that those who would have authority without vulnerability ultimately cannot be trusted with authority at all. In the end, the justice of God will abolish the authority of those who have purchased their power at the price of others' flourishing, those who refuse to enter into relationship with the God who is authority and vulnerability together. Very often, idols drag us down to hell on their own in this life. But if those who seem to end this life having sustained and benefited from tyranny are not ultimately brought to account, the world is the cruelest possible charade. If there is no hell for those who cling to tyranny and refuse mercy, there is no such thing as justice.

But if there is no mercy for those of us who have sought out and benefited from idols, no path out of their grip and back to the flourishing for which we are made, we are desperate people indeed.

INTERLUDE

The Path to Flourishing

What have we learned from this journey around the 2x2 grid?

We have ended up at the real root of the problem: the quest for authority without vulnerability. This quest, which began with our very first parents, haunts the human story and generates the axis of false choice, the line from Exploiting to Suffering, the only alternatives we have ever really known. We live in a world where sin has been, in the fullest sense, institutionalized—where for generation after generation, the privileged and powerful rule without risk, exposing others to the deepest vulnerability while excluding them from true authority. Exploiting and Suffering sum up the tragedy of our whole human history.

But this is not the way it was supposed to be. Our calling

is up and to the right. We are meant to experience more and more of the full authority intended for human beings, which can never be separated from the full vulnerability—the ultimate meaningful risk—of entrusting ourselves to one another and to our Creator.

Even in our sin-infested world we get glimpses of this story, too. A healthy human childhood is spent in Safety—protected from risk, not yet invested with authority. As we grow, our parents give us more and more authority, while also allowing us more and more exposure to risk. By portraying our first human parents in a divinely planted garden, Genesis suggests that the whole human drama was meant to follow the same pattern—from the protection and innocence of Eden to the full flourishing, multiplying and dominion that God intends for his image bearers. Safety to Flourishing is the way it was always meant to be.

How do we move from the story of Exploiting and Suffering to the story of Safety and Flourishing? How do we make space for the safety of childhood without retreating into the apathy of affluence? How do we elevate every member of our communities to the dignity and responsibility of image bearing without succumbing to the temptations of idolatry?

If you have started to ask these questions, you have already begun to be a leader.

Leadership does not begin with a title or a position. It

begins the moment you are concerned more about others' flourishing than you are about your own. It begins when you start to ask how you might help create and sustain the conditions for others to increase their authority and vulnerability together. In a world where many people simply withdraw into safety, where others are imprisoned in the most extreme vulnerability, where others pursue their own unaccountable authority, anyone who seeks true flourishing is already, in many senses, a leader. Isabel, the house cleaner in Santa Barbara whom we met in chapter three, is such a person. Her concern extends far beyond her own circumstances to those she serves, affluent homeowners and immigrant women alike.

Leadership begins the moment you are more concerned about others' flourishing than you are about your own.

Leaders like Isabel are preoccupied by much deeper questions than their own flourishing. They are asking questions about the flourishing of the vulnerable and the kinds of communities that contribute to the flourishing of the vulnerable. Leaders, you could say, lose interest in self-help books. They are no longer looking primarily to help themselves but to spend themselves on others. This does not mean they neglect personal growth—quite the opposite.

> Leadership begins the moment you are more concerned about others' flourishing than you are about your own.

Personal growth becomes more and more important as we realize how easily we get stuck in Suffering, Withdrawing or Exploiting and how little we contribute to Flourishing when we are mired in those corners. But personal growth now serves a different end—not our own satisfaction or fulfillment, but becoming the kind of people who could actually help others flourish. Our goal is to see others act meaningfully and take meaningful risks—to see both authority and vulnerability flourish in communities as small as a family or as large as a nation.

The good news is that we cannot, and do not have to, pull ourselves out of the mire of quadrants II, III and IV. We will not restore the world to its intended flourishing by impressive feats of self-improvement. Instead the restoration of the world flows from the singular life of a singular human being, Jesus, the only human being who could fully bear the burden or offer the gifts of what we so glibly call "leadership." It is only Jesus, and the Spirit he has sent to empower his people for their redemptive mission in creation, who truly sets us free from the mire of poverty, apathy and tyranny.

And so our liberation from the false quadrants is not the job of anyone other than Jesus. It is a work of sovereign redemption by the One who rescued us when we could not rescue ourselves. Any lasting progress toward the freedom and true power of Flourishing is a result of God's gracious activity in the world.

True transformation of the world, and ourselves, will only happen as we are conformed to the image of Jesus Christ—as his way becomes our way, his source of power becomes our source, and his patterns of life become our patterns.

But this leads us to two further paradoxical truths about flourishing—truths that flow directly from observing Jesus' transformative exercise of power in his brief years of public life. There are two places Jesus went where we, too, have to go. If we have truly absorbed the dangers of the false choices that have distorted our lives, communities and relationships, these will be the two places we least would expect to go and would least desire to go.

They are, oddly enough, versions of quadrant IV—authority without vulnerability—and quadrant II—vulnerability without authority. The very places we must choose to go are the very places human beings are not meant to go, the two ends of the axis of false choice—both of which we must visit, embrace and find emptied of their power by a power not our own.

If we want to be agents of transformation in the world, we must be willing to bear the burden of *visible* authority with *hidden* vulnerability. This will expose us to the temptation to become idols or tyrants ourselves—and yet without learning to bear hidden vulnerability, we will never truly be able to serve the flourishing of others.

And we also must choose the way of Suffering, exposing ourselves to vulnerability without authority—up to the ultimate experience of risk without the possibility of meaningful action, the land of the dead.

Only if we visit these two quadrants, in the right time and in the right way, will we bear the image of the most transformative human being the world has ever known.

Hidden Vulnerability

The most highly classified document in the United States government is called the President's Daily Brief. Usually delivered to the president in person each morning by the director of national intelligence, the brief summarizes the most critical information that the United States' vast network of intelligence agencies has learned in the previous twenty-four hours.

Of all the briefs prepared since the practice began in 1961, only two pages have ever been released to the public—an entry called "Bin Laden Determined To Strike in US" that was presented to the president on August 6, 2001.

Every morning, the president hears an unvarnished, detailed account of all the threats facing the country. Then comes the rest of the day's agenda. Ceremonies, meetings, phone calls, the occasional press conference, state dinners—and during them all, the president knows what almost no one else knows to the same degree of detail. And of all that troubling and terrifying knowledge, the president cannot speak a word.

The drama of leadership is hidden vulnerability.

With many kinds of flourishing, we see authority and vulnerability together—that is, we actually can see and perceive them. When we watch a great musician perform or a great athlete compete, we can hear the breathtaking complexity of the music or see the competitor just behind them. Our admiration comes from our keen awareness not just of the performers' authority but their vulnerability as well.

Sometimes, however, flourishing comes with *invisible* vulnerability—especially in leadership. Almost by definition, leaders have evident authority—but almost by definition, they also bear vulnerability that no one else can see. They may have access to more complete information than those they lead—as the president does after his morning briefing. They may simply possess deeper insight and intuition of the challenges they and their organizations face. This is what it is to be a leader: to bear the risks that only you can see, while continuing to exercise authority that everyone can see.

David is the founder and CEO of a technology startup company in San Diego. "I've learned that there is only one answer to the question, 'How is your business going?'" he told me recently. "It's one word long. 'Great.' Then, if they ask a follow-up question, you're allowed to have one more sentence, and that sentence has to be about how great it is—the latest product breakthrough, your last big hire. Then you have to stop." To say any more could affect how his customers, his investors, his suppliers and his own employees see the company. If they perceive it to be seriously vulnerable, there could be an unintended cascading decline of orders, investments and confidence.

> "There is only one answer to the question, 'How is your business going?'" he told me recently. "It's one word long. 'Great.'"

The truth is that for long stretches of the last few years, "great" did not really describe his business's precarious existence, let alone his own—perpetually a few days' income away from running out of money, lying awake at night wondering how he is going to meet the next payroll, losing critical employees at the worst times. Even as the firm has inched forward toward viability and profitability, as it has accumulated just enough authority to keep winning clients and closing additional funding rounds, at every point it has been out on a precarious ledge, one bad break away from total failure.

Twenty-nine employees rely on David's company to pay their mortgages and provide for their families and their futures. And David's own family and future are at stake, too. San Diego is a small city, where everyone in the business community knows everyone else. "My investors tell me that if this company fails, I'll never have a job in San Diego again," David tells me.

No pressure.

And through all of this, through the years of work that have strained his marriage, his health and his faith, he's had to give one answer when anyone asks how the business is going.

"Great."

This is not idolatry or injustice—not a case of someone hoarding authority and power and displacing vulnerability onto others. David is creating flourishing at real personal risk and cost. It hasn't been easy, but David is truly living "up and to the right." But David has discovered that even for healthy leaders, there is often a gap between public perception and private reality (see figure 6.1).

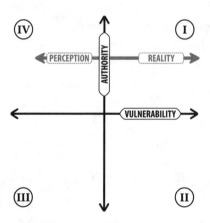

Figure 6.1. Healthy leadership

David's private reality is quadrant I—high authority matched with high vulnerability. But his public perception, at least among his employees and the business community, is largely in quadrant IV—authority higher than vulnerability. When the deepest truth of your life is quadrant I, but others assume you are in quadrant IV, you are probably, like it or not, a leader.

This doesn't just apply to organizational leaders, of course. It applies just as well to my friend Nate, father of two preschool children, who exclaimed to me, "It is amazing how such small creatures can make you so angry!" To his daughters, Nate no doubt appears almost pure authority. They cannot begin to imagine how much vulnerability he bears as their father, including the painful discovery of his own impatience and need for control. Anyone who takes responsibility for others' flourishing has probably discovered just how invisibly humbling even the most basic acts of care can be.

But the gap between perception and reality can also run the other way. What if leaders are perceived as more vulnerable, more exposed to meaningful risk, than they actually are? This is the essence of *manipulation* (see figure 6.2).

Manipulative leaders have learned to fake vulnerability—to seem exposed to risk and thus committed to flourishing. But in fact they use their ostensible vulnerability to shore

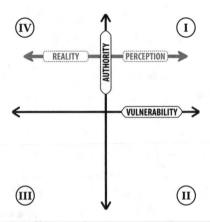

Figure 6.2. Manipulation

up unbalanced authority. These are leaders who can produce tears on command, who share carefully chosen heartfelt anecdotes of personal failure, who seem empathetic and kind—or leaders who call attention to every little threat to their power and constantly warn of the power of their enemies, while secretly consolidating their ability to control.

Such leaders, by being seen as more vulnerable than they are, conceal a powerful commitment to *invulnerability*. They can win sympathy and even loyalty with their calculated self-disclosures or complaints about their opponents. But leaders who use the appearance of vulnerability as a strategy to gain more authority are far less trustworthy than leaders who bear it truthfully but privately.

You surely have already spotted the danger here. How can a life of leadership that spans quadrant I and quadrant IV be a healthy one? Isn't quadrant IV the realm of idols and tyrants, the home of the most basic mistake we can make and the most ancient lie we can believe?

COMMUNITY VULNERABILITY

As risky as it is, hidden vulnerability is often necessary for true transformation. *The most important thing we are called to do is help our communities meet their deepest vulnerability with appropriate authority*—to help our communities live in the full authority and full vulnerability of Flourishing. And it turns out that in order to do that, we often must bear vulnerability that no one sees.

There are two kinds of vulnerability that must remain hidden if we are to lead others toward Flourishing. First, *the leader's own personal exposure to risk* must often remain unspoken, unseen and indeed unimagined by others. And second, *the leader must bear the shared vulnerabilities that the community does not currently have the authority to address.* Revealing either of these kinds of vulnerability will at best distract, and at worst paralyze, the community we are responsible for, robbing them of the opportunity for real flourishing. Because the community does not have the authority—the capacity for meaningful action—to deal with these vulnerabilities, asking the community to bear them will only plunge the community more deeply into Suffering.

Consider the two examples at the beginning of this chapter. Every morning the president is briefed on the full range of vulnerabilities that beset the nation. What would happen if this briefing were made public in all its terrifying detail? The truth is that if we all knew, every morning, what the president and his director of intelligence know, life as we know it would come to a halt. In an age of relentless broadcast and social media, even the most minor of dislocating events gets breathless attention. There are thirty thousand commercial plane flights in the United States every day—but should even a single plane crash, all attention is turned to that event. Why? Not just because of the loss of life—more lives are lost every day to automobile crashes, let alone to natural causes—but because airplane accidents are vivid reminders of the vulnerability, however small, of the plane travel that is a part of millions of people's lives.

As we saw earlier, human beings devote a disproportionate (though quite understandable) amount of their attention and energy to the possibility of loss, even when that comes at the expense of meaningful action. Imagine if every day we were exposed to the credible threats to our security that are dug up daily by the nation's vast intelligence network. We would, with some reason, have trouble thinking about or doing anything else. The nation would be consumed with fear and worse—prejudice, irrational hostility and frantic preparation. Even if we all had the full information that the president and his briefers know, there would be very little meaningful action most of us could take to avert the threat. (Not to mention the new threats that would arise from such sensitive information being made public.) We would be plunged deeply into Suffering—far more conscious of our vulnerability but equipped with no authority to meet it. Meanwhile, we would be distracted from the places—homes, neighborhoods, communities, businesses and organizations—where we do have an appropriate balance of authority and vulnerability and the real calling and capacity to act.

Think about David's startup company. What would happen if he began every day by unloading on his team the worries that had kept him up the night before? That disclosure might well make it impossible for any member of the team to focus on their work that day—the work that actually, in the long run, can increase the company's authority. In any case, much of what keeps David awake are matters that only a few people in the company actually have the capacity and responsibility to address. To disclose those vulnerabilities to the whole team is only to add to their vulnerability without adding anything to their authority. It is to take them deeper into Suffering, not up and to the right into Flourishing.

THE CALLING TO DIGNITY

This leads to a paradox that is often hard for privileged people to understand. The more a community experiences shared vulnerability without authority—the more that poverty and oppression have shaped a community's experience—the more likely that transformative leadership from within that community needs to bear hidden vulnerability.

I have had the great gift, at several seasons of my life, of worshiping and working in African American churches. It took me many years, as a young white man, to understand why leaders in the black church so often carry themselves with what initially seemed to me like excessive amounts of visible authority. A pastor wearing an expensive suit, driving a late-model car, and protected by layers of administrative staff and formality, presents very little apparent vulnerability to the world. Such leaders appear, especially to outsiders, as residents of something perilously close to the Exploiting quadrant. In middle-class and professional-class white churches, we expect more casual attire and emotionally transparent demeanor from our leaders.

But I gradually came to understand that black church leaders in fact bear a tremendous amount of vulnerability, even if it is not readily apparent. Their vulnerability can be personal: vanishingly few white Americans who drive late-model, high-end cars have ever been stopped by police

simply on suspicion that the vehicle is not theirs—whereas
many, many black pastors have experienced this insult to
their dignity and accomplishments. But more importantly,
as representatives of a historically subjugated community,
black pastors live every day bearing the nearly unbearable
burdens of a *community* that has been shaped by oppression and violence, prejudice and ignorance.

And the appropriate response to this hidden vulnerability is in fact public dignity—representing the community
not just in its vulnerability
but in its God-given,
image-bearing authority.
It may be appropriate for a
pastor in a privileged and
powerful community to
emphasize his vulnerability by saying, "Just call me Dan."
But it is entirely appropriate for a pastor in a community of
vulnerability to model authority and expect to be addressed,
especially in public, with his full title and family name.

> The appropriate response
> to this hidden vulnerability
> is in fact public dignity.

To be sure, there can be exploitative leaders in the black
church just as there are in every social system—very much
including the white church, where leaders can use transparency and modesty as a cloak for manipulation. But
healthy leadership in a context of oppression often requires
levels of visible authority that might seem unhealthy else-
where. What brings transforming hope in that context of

suffering is the presence of leaders who balance the *community's* vulnerability with their own *representative* authority. And when you truly get to know the most faithful and courageous leaders in the black church or any minority community, you come to understand that in contexts of oppression, authority is itself a great risk and a most vulnerable calling.

MISLEADING INTRODUCTIONS

One of the rituals associated with public speaking is the "introduction," in which hosts do their best to honor the invited speaker—and perhaps persuade the audience that the coming presentation will be worth their time and attention. As a result, when I step on stage to speak, someone has often gone to great lengths to present me as capable of meaningful action. Very rarely do they mention a single vulnerability. My introductions frequently mention my current employment—no one ever mentions that I lost a job (and a fair amount of investors' money) fifteen years before. They often mention my wife and family—no one ever mentions my failed romantic relationships in college and early adulthood. They frequently note my published books—without ever noting that my first two books were turned in years late thanks to procrastination, perfectionism, spiritual warfare and personal cowardice.

Nothing in the introduction prepares my audience to

see me, to whatever extent I may be so, as someone who dwells with *both* authority and vulnerability. All of it paints me, quite unrealistically, with pure authority. (Sometimes to the point of outright inaccuracy, as when I am introduced, despite my lack of a doctoral degree, as "Dr. Crouch.") When I step on stage, no one in the room is thinking about my exposure to risk—except me. As I wait to speak, and while I am speaking, if I am not disciplined and careful, my mind races to my various vulnerabilities in that moment. I am exquisitely conscious of the risks I am taking—even though with rare exceptions, no one else in the room registers them at all.

Not long ago I bought a new pair of dress shoes and wore them for the first time on stage. As the warm and flattering introduction came to a close, I rose from my chair—and felt the brand-new, slippery sole of my left shoe nearly skate away from me on the stage's polished hardwood. No one in the room realized I had nearly taken an inglorious tumble—but for the next twenty minutes, I was keenly aware of every step. The audience knew nothing of that vulnerability. Even less did they imagine the vulnerabilities in my life, as in every life, of far longer duration and far greater depth—the broken relationships, the deep disappointments, the persistent sins. But all of these come with me into every moment of leadership, no matter how much authority I am given.

And this is absolutely as it must be. Because if any of us, let alone those entrusted with leadership, showed up and were completely transparent about all the dimensions of vulnerability in our lives, nothing else would get done, any more than if every citizen knew of every threat to the nation's welfare. Were I to offer every audience a full accounting of the present, past and future exposure to loss in my life, I would be nothing but a distraction.

For one thing, these audiences have no authority in these vulnerabilities—no capacity for meaningful action to address them. Others in my life do have that authority—my supervisor, my friends, my confessors, my wife. But a hall full of strangers could only listen, with sympathy or alarm, to the reality of my—or anyone's—broken life.

But there is another, deeper reason that an endless parade of personal vulnerability would be the opposite of leadership at these times. When I am speaking, my deepest calling is to help a community bear *the community's* vulnerability. Every person in the room has their own litany of difficulties, dangers and doubts, and to serve them well is to directly or indirectly address *those* realities, not whatever may be preoccupying me on that particular day.

None of this means that leaders, whatever their cultural context, must be impenetrable fortresses of false authority. It certainly does not mean that leaders never expose their communities to the reality of the risks they face and the losses they must bear. It just means that when leaders take risks, including the risks of personal disclosure, they do so *for the sake of others' authority and proper vulnerability.* This is one sense in which leadership is always servanthood—it is always about others' flourishing, not our own, and it is always directed toward others' authority, not our own.

Make no mistake: transformational leadership helps people see and address real vulnerability. But leaders exist to match that vulnerability, as much as possible, with commensurate authority. So our job is often to increase others' authority while gradually, in a measured and intentional way, alerting them to vulnerabilities (including our own limitations, foibles and blindness). In the meantime, we must bear vulnerability that others cannot see, and sometimes will never see. Hidden vulnerability is the price of leadership.

Or as Max De Pree likes to say, "Bad leaders inflict pain. Good leaders bear it."

BURNOUT

This is a dangerous business. A public identity that emphasizes authority over vulnerability—even when we know just how vulnerable we and our communities are—is constantly in danger of sliding into idolatry and injustice. Institutions and communities constantly hope, if not demand, that their leaders assure them that they, too, can live with the kind of invulnerability they imagine their leaders possess. At its worst, leadership becomes an exercise in mutual deception, with both leader and community assuring one another that they have no vulnerability to bear, that authority without vulnerability is possible.

But the gap between public and private can take forms that are even more perilous. Often the public perception is not just of less vulnerability than the leader actually bears, but also of *more authority*. Others see us as living in quadrant IV, but in fact we know that our true reality is much more like Suffering (see figure 6.3).

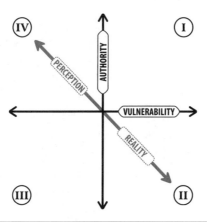

Figure 6.3. Burnout

Very often, leaders have far less real authority than others imagine. The seemingly powerful chief executive has been put on notice by her board that she is one quarter's results away from being fired. The pastor who preaches powerful sermons in fact has entirely lost touch with prayer, solitude and grace—the sources of true spiritual authority— and is consumed with lust, fear or bitterness. The universally beloved actor is unable to control a consuming and isolating addiction.

If only these were generic examples—but there are real names for every one of these and more. One of the more ironic photographs ever published in the pages of *Christianity Today* was of then-megachurch-pastor Ted Haggard in a hotel room in Denver, Colorado. Haggard, the caption informed readers, had been urged by his staff to get away from the busyness of daily ministry in order to write and prepare his sermons. The image in the magazine was of a leader seeking solitude and contemplation to serve his growing flock and national audience.

But within a year, a masseur and sometime prostitute in Denver claimed that he had been called by Haggard to hotel rooms just like that one. The revelations that followed, and Haggard's eventual acknowledgment of many of the accusations against him, overturned Haggard's ministry, ended his presidency of the National Association of Evangelicals and shook the faith of countless followers. Haggard's vulnerabilities were far deeper than anyone knew—but that is true for every single human being. What was really eroding, far faster than anyone guessed, was his authority, his capacity to live faithfully with those vulnerabilities.

When our perceived authority is completely out of step with our actual vulnerability—when there is no one who knows the true reality of our private life of suffering or flourishing—we are at the edge of burnout. Burnout does not just afflict popular and visible leaders. No one who has stepped into the story of this broken world is exempt— burnout is a risk for anyone who cares for others' flourishing. It emerges from our deepest callings and giftedness, but it feeds on our deepest brokenness. When people praise our commitment to a needy child, a chronically ill spouse or an underserved community, but we have no one who knows the depths of our fatigue, disappointment or despair, the gap between authority and vulnerability can become overwhelming. Indeed, public recognition of our authority and praise for our faithfulness can actually be fuel for the fire of burnout, compounding our sense of isolation in our loneliness and need.

The only question is how the story will end.

He Refused to Go In

In my eighth year of campus ministry at Harvard, the students decided to throw a party for me and for our ministry's coleader, Ming. Our campus fellowship ended each year with a weeklong leadership retreat after the end of final exams. These "chapter camps" were intense, rich experiences of study, worship, prayer and fellowship. They could also be surprisingly tiring for those of us responsible for leading them. A week of life together tends to expose vulnerabilities that would go unnoticed in less intense environments.

For whatever reason, in the course of that particular week, I had begun to feel the signs of burnout. I had joined this campus ministry as an outsider, a status accentuated by the insular culture of Harvard College. (I remember a friendly dinner conversation in my early years of ministry during which a student discovered that I had not gone to Harvard and in innocent surprise said, "That's funny—you *seem* smart!") After eight years I was completely accepted as a member of the community, but those early insecurities and frustrations lingered.

Then there were all the accumulated small griefs. In campus ministry, if everything goes as well as you could ever hope, your most beloved students, now in many ways your friends, leave after four years, rarely ever returning to your life. And everything does not by any means go as well as you hope. Along with the extraordinary joys of campus ministry—still to this day the most satisfying work of my life—had come conflicts, disappointments, disagreements, challenges to my authority, knowing or unknowing jabs at my own areas of vulnerability. None of this was unusual—none of it was unbearable. But all of it, after two full generations of students had come and gone, was wearing me down.

The students planned a party for Thursday night at 10:00 p.m., after the other scheduled activities were over—an event with only one agenda, to thank Ming and me for our leadership of the fellowship over the past year and to lift us up in prayer. It was supposed to be a surprise, but I got wind of the secret early Thursday morning. And in the course of the day, as unacknowledged resentments and discouragement bubbled up to the surface, I began forming a bitter plan, one I barely admitted even to myself that I was forming.

I would not go.

That night, I would go back to my room, dress for bed, turn out the lights and go to sleep, party be damned. My wife and I had a private cabin. No one would bother me there, far back in the woods, if the lights were out. Since the party was supposed to be a surprise, no one would know I was deliberately avoiding it. At some point they would give up, celebrate without me, and let me sleep through the night in my undisturbed loneliness.

Ten o'clock came and went. I lay in our bed, resentful and relieved. I was going to escape being celebrated, escape being thanked, escape having to see my students' love and gratitude. And escaping all that, I would be able to hold on to my frustration, justifying my emotional withdrawal even as I continued to go through the motions of leadership. Burned out and bitter, I was heading deep into the corner of quadrant III of Withdrawing, preparing to sleep like the untouchable dead. Party be damned, indeed.

But I had not counted on the persistence of my wife, Catherine. She was there waiting for the party to start, and as the appointed hour came and went she realized something was wrong. She walked down the lane to our cabin and opened the door. I considered simply feigning the deepest of sleep. But the second time she called my name I answered.

"Andy, you don't know about this"—she, like everyone else, had no idea how well I knew—"but there's a party for you and Ming right now. You have to come."

And then Catherine got one of her early, clear glimpses of the hardness of my heart.

"No. I'm not coming. Tell them I've gone to bed."

She was shocked. "They've been planning this all week. Everyone is waiting." This only made me even more embarrassed and determined.

"I'm not going to go." Now she could hear the bitterness in my voice, the distant retreat born of unjustifiable rage.

"You have to go," she said. And here is where my wife exercised both authority and vulnerability—because as she pleaded with me, she both came close to tears and became more and more insistent. She would not let me stay there in my petty and ungrateful pain. She won the argument, and in some sense she probably saved my life.

I got dressed, walked up the road to the main building, and as I came through the door the room erupted into cheers. No one knew where I had been or why I was late—they just knew that now that I had arrived, they could begin to celebrate. The party began.

I have had a few moments of sheer grace in my life—utterly undeserved, unmerited, unjustified abundance. That party, which went on so completely irrespective of my own best efforts to undermine it, was a foretaste of heaven, the party planned under our noses as we tried our best to destroy it. It was as if the older son in Jesus' parable of the prodigal had decided to go in after all, and it turned out that everything was planned for him all along. At the end of the night the students gave Ming and me countless envelopes of notes of thanks, full of tenderness and kindness—I have them within reach as I sit writing, nearly twenty years later, in a folder simply labeled "Encouragement." I suppose it could also be labeled "Flourishing."

JESUS' HIDDEN VULNERABILITY

Of every human being who has ever lived, Jesus lived most completely in the fullness of authority and vulnerability.

His authority was evident to everyone—at every turn of the gospel narratives we see Jesus exercising unparalleled capacity for meaningful action as well as restoring authority to the marginal and poor.

But no one fully grasped Jesus' vulnerability. Those around him comprehended almost nothing of his true purpose and destination. The gospel writers report that even when Jesus began to try to explain to his disciples the fate he knew awaited him in Jerusalem, they resisted and did not understand. As his ministry brought him nearer and nearer to the final confrontation with the forces of idolatry and injustice, only Jesus understood what was truly going to be lost.

We see Jesus gradually explaining his vulnerability to his disciples. He predicts his arrest and death three times. When he is anointed by the woman in Simon's house, an act that any Israelite would have assumed was a sign of kingship—a proclamation of authority—he reinterprets her lavish gift as preparation for his burial—a recognition of vulnerability. When he gathers them for dinner the night before his arrest, he speaks of his body and blood and the dark truth that he will be betrayed by a member of the apostles' inner circle. But none of this seems to have truly penetrated the minds or imaginations of his companions— at least not his male companions. They remain fixated on the dreams of a Messiah who would deliver Israel, freed from their enemies and returned to rightful possession of their land. Even at the moment of Jesus' arrest in the garden, one of his followers resorts to a burst of violence to ward off the approaching doom.

Jesus bore not only his own knowledge of his own personal fate, but a clear knowledge of the risks hanging over the city of Jerusalem—the knowledge that one generation later, the city would be razed to the ground as the Romans put down Jewish rebellion once and for all. This knowledge, too, he shared with his disciples, but the full weight of it fell on Jesus alone. Beyond the fate of people, land and temple, we may suppose that even the very human Jesus of Nazareth had some grasp of the full exposure to loss of the One who was very God—the comprehension of the full rebellion in every time, place and cosmic dimension against the Word through whom all things were made, a rebellion that could only be redeemed by his own substitution and sacrifice.

We see Jesus' authority and vulnerability come together in a most astonishing way in the scene we call the transfiguration, when Jesus took his three closest followers with him, went up a mountain and was changed before them into a being of dazzling glory, accompanied by Moses and Elijah. This might seem like a scene of pure authority, and so the church has usually interpreted it. But it is much more than that. Luke tells us what the three powerful figures were discussing: "his departure, which he was about to accomplish at Jerusalem" (Luke 9:31). They speak together, not about Jesus' power, but about his impending condemnation and crucifixion.

At a moment when his own followers are clueless, Jesus speaks with two of Israel's greatest leaders, Moses and Elijah, about the greatest risk of his or any life. What is revealed on the mountain of the transfiguration is not authority alone, but authority with vulnerability, power with self-denial, divinity with humanity—unconquerable life and imminent death.

Was the transfiguration a set piece staged for the benefit of Peter, James and John? That hardly seems likely, given that they were barely awake, confused and uncomprehending. Much more likely, the transfiguration reveals the absolute necessity of communion with others to sustain a life of flourishing. Jesus, who regularly sought out communion with his Father, went up a high mountain to seek the human companionship of those who, like him, had borne authority and vulnerability on behalf of Israel, who could foresee clearly with him what his own followers could not, who could speak with him of the risks he was choosing to bear and strengthen him for his final journey to the city he loved and wept over.

It is dangerous to draw any simple parallels between this extraordinary story and our own small lives, but it reminds us of at least one universal truth: no one survives hidden vulnerability without companions who understand. No one can turn hidden vulnerability into flourishing without friends. We will never be able to fully reveal our vulnerability to the wide world— but we will never survive it without companions willing to bear it with us.

> No one can turn hidden vulnerability into flourishing without friends.

The transfiguration, along with everything that followed, now leads us to the other great, paradoxical theme in the lives of those who would bring flourishing into the world. We are called to risk hidden vulnerability, finding a way to bear authority without becoming an idol or tyrant. But we are also called to very visible suffering, to journey to the quadrant down and to the right—to descend to the dead.

DESCENDING TO THE DEAD

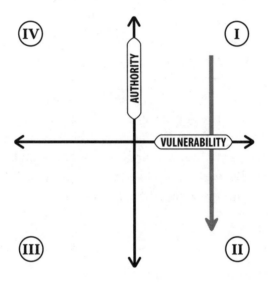

Without a doubt, this is the greatest paradox of flourishing: it is only found on the other side of suffering—specifically, our willingness to actively embrace suffering. The marriage of authority and vulnerability, which is our glad destiny as image bearers, is only possible if we are willing to bear vulnerability without authority.

Our mission in the world is to help individuals and whole communities—ultimately, all humanity—move up and to the right. But to do so, especially to set free those who have suffered the most from idolatry, addiction, injustice and tyranny, requires us to go where no one wants to go: voluntary exposure to pain and loss.

Why is this necessary? Because of the extraordinary grip of idols over our world.

The idols are all the forces that whisper the promises of control, invulnerable power and independence—and then, having seduced us with those promises, enslave us to their demands and blind us with their distorted view of the world. We have been so completely conquered by idols' lies—we are so enslaved to their domination—that we cannot truly comprehend, let alone attain, a life that is as exposed to meaningful risk as it is capable of meaningful action.

In a healthy world, every increase in authority, every move upward, would be matched by an increase in risk, a move to the right. This is the pattern that would keep us dependent on God and one another, empowering others rather than hoarding our power, and discovering new dimensions of flourishing. But in the world as we know it, acts of authority frequently insulate us from risk rather than opening us up to it. Something is warped in the grain of the universe, something that prevents us from turning authority into flourishing—we are bent in the direction of exploitation, privilege and safety. Such is the power of the lies that have insinuated themselves into the human story from the very beginning.

All of us are afflicted by the forces of idolatry and injustice, but when we take responsibility for others' flourishing we become even more exposed to the power of these forces. Even when leaders do bear real vulnerability, as we saw in the last chapter, it is necessarily hidden from others much of the time. Even when—perhaps especially when— leaders are at their most vulnerable, the rest of us persist in seeing them as invulnerable. We want to see them that way—we need to see them that way, lest we face the true reality of our own vulnerability. No matter how much leaders pursue integrity and flourishing, the forces preventing their true vulnerability from being seen are deep and powerful. Indeed, it is not too strong to say that those forces are demonic. Every leader and every community, whether we like it or not, is implicated in the cosmic rebellion that denies that vulnerability leads to flourishing.

What could truly break the power of that rebellion? If someone were to dramatically empty himself of authority, voluntarily give up the capacity for meaningful action, be handed over to the most exploitative forces in our cosmos, and go to the land of the dead, the realm of those who have lost all capacity for action—and if that same person were to return, rescued, fully alive, indeed with far more authority than we had ever seen or imagined—such a complete sacrifice, and victory, might conclusively unmask the lie that is at the heart of all exploitation.

In the wake of such a sacrifice and such a triumph, human beings might be set free from their fantasies of authority without vulnerability. They would see with their own eyes, and touch with their hands, the evidence that God's power is greater even than death—they would know that nothing, and no one, can ever be ultimately lost when God acts to rescue and restore. Even very ordinary people who witnessed such an emptying, reversal and vindication might find themselves with authority no one could imagine they could ever have possessed, with a boldness to risk that was unprecedented even in their own histories. They might find themselves swept into the very courtyards, courts and courtrooms where the world's idols hold sway, brought into the presence of the most powerful representatives of the whole cosmic system of exploitation, conducting themselves with utter authority and serenity. They might become the agents of a gradual but inexorable overthrow of the idols and their lies, even when those idols did their best to do their worst, consigning these representatives of true flourishing to torture and death.

Such people might begin to turn the world upside down.

KING'S CROSS

There is an ancient phrase in the Apostles' Creed that is odd enough that some Christians, and some churches, omit it altogether: *descendit ad inferos,* "he descended to the dead" or more vividly, "he descended into hell." It recalls the Hebrew idea of Sheol, the country of the dead. Early on, Christians came to believe that on Holy Saturday, the day between Good Friday and Easter, Christ somehow journeyed to that realm to set free the "spirits in prison" (1 Peter 3:19), extending the benefits of his resurrection to those who had lived and died long before. The Orthodox have an icon called the Harrowing of Hell that shows Jesus, triumphant over death, grasping the arms of Adam and Eve—in most versions of the icon they look rather startled— and lifting them out of their graves.

Whatever exactly took place on Holy Saturday, that most solemn of sabbaths, the day itself is as crucial to the full truth of Jesus' lordship as Good Friday and Easter Sunday. There is a gap—on that first Saturday, it would have felt more like a chasm—between Jesus' death and his resurrection. Two nights pass without any apparent hope. His body lies cold in the tomb; his friends shiver in their total exposure to vulnerability. Jesus drains the cup of wrath to its dregs. He does not just take one taste of death, spit it out and fly up to heaven. He descends to the dead, and there, for all that his disciples can see or know from Friday to Sunday, he stays.

There is something deep in the human heart that knows that the last enemy to be conquered is death. Death is the last enemy not just because it takes life but because the fear of death prevents real life. The fear of loss has robbed our world of more life and more flourishing than any actual loss we could ever suffer.

But death is not just a mirage. Loss is real, the risk of loss is real, and vulnerability is real. Those who try to wish away loss, to promise action without risk and life without vulnerability, participate themselves in the very destructive system that ensures suffering, loss and death. Only those who have faced loss, who have drunk from the cup of undiluted vulnerability—and who have been rescued by a power infinitely beyond their own at the depths of their greatest need—can offer hope stronger than the idol's word of fear.

The descent to the dead finds its way into the myths that shape our culture—and, probably, every culture. In our lighter entertainment, we may settle for heroes who only *seem* to die—no movie is complete without the penultimate moment of despair when it seems that all is lost, followed by the inevitable though surprising reversal that leads to victory. But our most compelling stories—the archetypal tales that shape our deepest hopes and fears—recognize that mere peril is not enough for real heroism. Not until someone has actually sacrificed everything, drained the cup and returned to tell the tale, can we believe that real victory has been won.

J. K. Rowling's Harry Potter series, so lighthearted in its early books, takes its hero in the climax of the sixth book to a cave with his beloved mentor Albus Dumbledore, where Harry must force Dumbledore to drink ten times from a poisoned goblet. Then they ascend to the parapet of Hogwarts, where Dumbledore commands his own murder in order to save the life, and very possibly the soul, of one of the books' most despicable characters. In the seventh book it is Harry himself who must give himself up to death. On the other side of that sacrifice he encounters Dumbledore again in an otherworldly version of the train station named King's Cross. The most beloved children's books of our time—or perhaps any time—are unflinching in their understanding that true happy endings are won only at the greatest cost and that no king is truly a king without a cross.

So the phrase *descendit ad inferos* not only says something important about the extent of Jesus' redemptive suffering—how deeply he participated in human loss, how far his saving power extends—but also about the nature of Christlike life and leadership. Only

> True happy endings are won only at the greatest cost. No king is truly a king without a cross.

those who have descended to the dead can be fully trusted to lead—because only they can truly declare vanquished the fear that animates all idolatry and exploitation.

How to Descend

"It was the spring semester of the academic year, and I was in trouble." Those were the opening words of President Philip Ryken's convocation address at Wheaton College on August 27, 2014—the first chapel service of the fall. Ryken was not referring to a time of difficulty from some distant spring semester during his own student years. Instead, in an address titled, "Nobody Knows the Trouble I've Seen," he described his descent into a deep depression just a few months before, to the point where "I wondered if I had the will to live."

Convocation at Wheaton is a formal affair, and Ryken wore the academic robes that signaled his academic training and his office—the signs of authority. Like the Presbyterian pastor that he is, he read a thoughtfully composed address from a manuscript. But the content of his address was the raw experience of someone who has entered into the darkest night of the soul, only emerging thanks to the persistent love of family and friends and the grace of God. "Now that I'm giving this address," he joked, "maybe I should title it 'Everybody Knows the Trouble I've Seen.'"

For any of us, let alone a college president, to speak so candidly about our darkest moments would be a considerable risk. And yet in the months after that address, every time I spoke with a member of the Wheaton community about themes of healthy leadership and authority, they brought up Ryken's unforced honesty. It had made him a different, better kind of leader—and it had made the college a different, better kind of community.

Nineteen million people have viewed the TEDx Houston talk that made Brené Brown a household name (at least in households that watch TED talks). It begins engagingly enough, with Brown narrating how her research for a PhD in social work began to focus on the question of why some people are so "whole-hearted" even in the face of great adversity—able to sustain a sense of love and belonging. But ten minutes in the talk takes a remarkable turn, as Brown describes the way she began to personally pursue the kind of vulnerability she was discovering in her healthiest subjects. Suddenly we are hearing not just wise words from an experienced researcher, but the raw and wry confession of a fellow human being. "The definition of research is to control and predict—and now my mission to control and predict had turned up the answer that the way to live is with vulnerability and to stop controlling and predicting," she told the audience. "This led to a little breakdown—I call it a breakdown; my therapist calls it a spiritual awakening."

The outpouring of admiration and affection that has followed Brown's talk is a sign of what so many people are hungry for—not just the expertise she wields so deftly, but the honesty she offers so freely.

My friend Jim is a tenured professor in a department at a major research university where most faculty are more feared than loved. Yet Jim is admired and indeed beloved by the graduate students he supervises. Thanks in part to his talents, his character and his simple good fortune, failure and loss have been a remarkably small part of his life. But they are a huge part of his influence. "I've learned a lot over the years about how to be focused and effective in my work. When I share ways to manage time well or make effective career decisions, my students politely say they find it helpful," he told me somewhat ruefully. "But what really seems to matter to them is when I share my failures." Somehow, knowing that such an accomplished person nonetheless experiences disappointment and frustration turns out to be more empowering than simply knowing his secrets for success.

Each of these people has found—or stumbled upon— the paradox of flourishing. The most transformative acts of our lives are likely to be the moments when we radically empty ourselves, in the very settings where we would normally be expected to exercise authority. As Jim has discovered, his competence is helpful—but his vulnerability is transformative. This is not the manipulative vulnerability that primarily benefits the person already in power, but an unforced gift of truthfulness. Descending to the dead, embracing a position of unequivocal vulnerability, accomplishes something nothing else can.

These moments of descent *ad inferos* are necessarily rare. It would be odd, and not ultimately fruitful, for the president of Wheaton College to give an annual chapel address disclosing his deepest personal distress from the past year; it would be self-indulgent for a tenured professor to constantly regale his students with accounts of his failures. (Regular viewers of TED talks can judge for themselves whether the touching personal disclosure at the ten-minute mark has, since Brené Brown's talk went viral, become an expected cliché rather than a genuine sacrifice.) The kind of vulnerability we are called to on a day-to-day basis is far more prosaic—and in its way more demanding—and we will examine it in the next chapter.

But communities also need people who are willing to move decisively down and to the right, surrendering authority while taking up unusual vulnerability. Ronald Heifetz, who has taught a highly regarded course on leadership at Harvard's Kennedy School of Government for several decades, observes that the primary responsibility of every leader is to avoid assassination. True enough. Quite aside from the upheaval that assassination introduces into any nation or organization, an assassinated leader is obviously of no further use. Heifetz is simply observing that leaders must take care to preserve their authority, their capacity for action—which requires, at a minimum, remaining alive—even while they lead their communities into appropriate vulnerability.

But a more accurate version of Heifetz's dictum would be this: you only get to be assassinated once. So as far as possible, the ultimate responsibility of a leader is to choose wisely and well the form and timing of that descent. Indeed, someone who is not ready to descend to the dead—to hand over all authority and embrace maximum vulnerability—is almost certainly in the grip of idolatry. After all, there is another word for someone who will never give up power, especially one who devotes more and more energy to avoiding assassination: a dictator. We might amend Heifetz this way: the primary responsibility of every leader is to prepare and plan for their descent to the dead.

Sometimes we get more than one opportunity to dramatically and publicly embrace vulnerability. Nelson Mandela, a leader of the armed resistance movement in South Africa called the African National Congress (ANC), had his first moment of descent to the dead when he was convicted of treason and sentenced to prison on Robben Island, the prison compound located on an island nine cruel miles from Cape Town. It was there, stripped of his authority, that Mandela became convinced (and began to convince others) that the ANC had to find a way to make peace, with justice, with the apartheid regime. In the exile of suffering, he acquired a spiritual authority he would never have found any other way. And when, against all odds, apartheid ended and Mandela was elected president of the new South Africa, he made yet another dramatic decision to empty himself of authority, standing down from his position as president after just one term in order to establish a precedent of peaceful, just transitions of power. Of all the powerful things Mandela did, voluntarily giving up power may have been the most transformative and consequential for the nation that had come to call him "Tata Mandela," the nation's father.

DYING AS LEADING
How can we "descend to the dead," embracing suffering in dramatic and transformative ways?

Dying. In some times and places, we do so by being willing to literally die. As I was preparing this book for publication, a young man entered the basement of "Mother Emanuel" AME Church in Charleston, South Carolina, sat through nearly an hour of the Wednesday night Bible study, and then took the lives of nine people, including the church's senior pastor, the Reverend Clementa Pinckney. Reverend Pinckney was forty-one years old, a respected state senator and beloved servant of the church, the embodiment of authority used well. But on that night he became something greater, more holy and more terrible— a martyr for the long-suffering black church and its witness to grace and truth in the face of injustice and racism. Along with him were eight others, ranging in age from twenty-six to eighty-seven. Some of them were ordained ministers with positions of leadership; others were not. But in those awful moments, all of them joined the cloud of witnesses to God's faithfulness in the face of evil.

Commenting on the martyrdom of the Charleston Nine and the subsequent faithfulness of the surviving congregation, the Episcopal priest and writer Fleming Rutledge said, "They were not ready"—how could anyone be ready for such sudden and gratuitous violence?—"but they were prepared." When evil came into their midst, the church members in the basement responded instinctively with sacrifice, some of them placing themselves between the killer and his intended victims even while pleading with him to reconsider his plans—and when their surviving family members confronted the killer in a court hearing just two days after the murders, they responded with offers of mercy and even salvation in the face of his impending judgment.

No one of us can be ready for moments like this—instead, we must, long before, train ourselves in the image of Christ to be prepared should such a time come. Because the Charleston Nine, their families and their church were prepared, what was intended for utmost evil became the most astonishing witness to the power of the gospel in American public life in many years and also dealt a powerful blow to the hold of racism over the institutions and symbols of the American South.

It is mercifully unlikely that most of us will face the stark evil that confronted the Charleston Nine that night or that confronts faithful people in many parts of the world today. Yet all of us will come to the end of our lives, and the way we approach that end may give us opportunities to become influential in ways we never imagined, in ways that break the power of idols that hold our communities captive. Indeed, if we are not prepared to die in the presence of others, we are probably missing out on the deep community for which we, and they, are made.

My last book was dedicated to our neighbor and friend David Sacks, a photographer, musician and father whose suffering and death from cancer at age forty-six became, against all odds, an extraordinary testimony to community, faithfulness and life in ways that indelibly touched thousands of people in our corner of Pennsylvania and beyond. And this book is dedicated to Steve Hayner, who was in the middle of an assignment as president of Columbia Theological Seminary when he was diagnosed with pancreatic cancer. Steve and his wife, Sharol, lived, as presidents do, in a house owned by the seminary. Shortly before Steve was selected as president, the seminary had had a first-floor bathroom and bedroom suite installed in the president's house. The renovations were designed to accommodate some future president who might fall ill, Steve told friends, "but I never imagined I would be the president to die in this house." Nine months after his initial diagnosis, he did die in that house. But before his death, Steve and Sharol wrote a series of short updates online, as well as countless personal notes to family and friends, that were unflinching in their honesty and hope. Steve descended to the dead, but not without leaving behind a testimony to God's grace in the midst of suffering and loss and a house made holy by the grief and hope of his last days.

Relinquishing power. Like Nelson Mandela, every leader needs a plan for how to lay down their authority once and for all. As with Mandela, many leaders need to plan to lay that power aside *before* their own communities would expect or demand it. It is hard to think of many things that do more damage to an organization than leaders who have no plan for how they will hand over power. No leader lives forever, and few leaders can or should, like Steve, lead until the end of their natural lives. This responsibility is not just the leader's own—it is the responsibility of the whole community to envision and plan for life beyond their current leader's tenure. When leaders do not actively plan for the end of their power, and when we who are led by them allow them to indulge fantasies of unending influence, they are idols, no matter how well disguised.

Confessing sin. In one sense, confession is the routine task of every Christian. It should be as natural as breathing for us to admit fault and ask for forgiveness, part of the constant dance between authority and vulnerability that leads us all to flourishing. But there are also times to make a more dramatic confession, especially when vulnerability has been hidden and concealed for too long. In the last chapter I told the story of the party I desperately tried to avoid and the grace that was poured out in spite of my bitterness. That night, no one knew how hard I had tried to escape that gift of grace. But the next day, I knew I had to tell that community the whole, painful, humbling truth. There is something indescribably painful about having just been celebrated and affirmed and then having to reveal just how unworthy of celebration and affirmation you truly are—and yet to do so is also utterly right and safe and joyful. That next morning, after I had confessed my utter failure, I felt as known and loved as I ever have in my life. I would not trade that moment for anything—even the celebration the night before.

Dying, relinquishing power, confessing sin, receiving and offering forgiveness—these are all indispensable ways that we can descend to the dead. In doing so we not only break the grip of idols; we restore the kinds of relationships, especially with the most vulnerable, that the idols have destroyed.

But sometimes it is even simpler. Sometimes you just have to walk.

Los Gringos Que Caminan

In the 1990s a group of Peruvian lawyers founded an organization called Paz y Esperanza (known in English as Peace and Hope International) to address the countless injustices committed by both sides in the Shining Path insurgency. Over time, with painstaking effort and frequently slow progress, Paz y Esperanza has made significant contributions to flourishing and the rule of law in several Latin American countries.

Drew Jennings-Grisham is an American who joined Paz y Esperanza in 2001 to help expand the organization's work in Bolivia. The gospel has been widely preached in Bolivia, but most indigenous communities had remained dependent initially on white missionaries, and then on missionaries from more empowered urban churches, and lacked their own leaders and pastors. Fresh out of college, Jennings-Grisham found that even a twenty-something American would be granted absurd amounts of authority. "They see a white guy with a Bible coming into their community, and they give me the visible and spiritual authority. They've never seen me before, don't know me from Adam, but as soon as I step into that situation, I'm the one with the power, because that had been their experiences with the missionaries and even with the urban Bolivian churches."

So Jennings-Grisham embraced ever more dramatic symbolic ways of sharing the vulnerability of his indigenous hosts, who also became his friends. He eschewed the usual trappings of Western-funded missionaries like hotel rooms and the air-conditioned white SUVs that are the mark of spiritual and secular NGOs around the world.

> We would spend the night on the street as we traveled, sleeping on the sidewalk with a blanket. I wouldn't bring any food with me except what I brought as my common contribution to the group. The Ayoreo people we were traveling with were destitute—they ate rice, one meal a day. One Ayoreo pastor told me, "When we saw you eating our rice, with maggots in it, we knew you were different." All I was trying to do is, as a person with power, to say, *I'm completely powerless right now. If you left me here I'd get lost and starve to death. If we get lost in this jungle, you guys will be fine, but I'll be dead in twelve hours.*

Just as representatives of highly vulnerable communities are right to clothe themselves in visible symbols of authority, so when representatives of unearned authority—

say, "a white guy with a Bible"—enter into settings of historic oppression and injustice, we must go out of our way to clothe ourselves in visible symbols of vulnerability. Of course, Jennings-Grisham and other Westerners could simply decide never to visit Bolivia at all—never to risk the complications of facing, stewarding and giving away their power. But to do so would leave patterns of injustice untouched and unchallenged. Far more challenging, but far more fruitful, is to enter into relationships where we can learn what it means both to lead and to serve, where both the possessors of privilege and the putatively powerless can discover greater flourishing together.

So Jennings-Grisham also became known as the *gringo* who would walk out of meetings—not in frustration or anger, but so that his presence would not influence the decisions being made. "We started one meeting sitting at a table, in the way urban Bolivians and Westerners do," one of his colleagues told me,

> but at a certain point in the meeting, Drew stood up, asked all the Westerners and the urbanized Bolivians to unplug their laptops and leave the room with him. You can imagine that made the urbanized Bolivians a bit nervous! Drew said, "We're going to get lunch for the group—you talk this over and make the decision." When we came back a few hours later, the indigenous leaders had moved the table out of the way, sat down

in a circle, and come to a conclusion. The result, a few months later, was a church conference, probably the first in the history of the country, that was planned and led by indigenous Bolivians.

Jennings-Grisham is back in the United States now, building relationships between the American and Bolivian church. Back in Bolivia, he and his wife are remembered with a simple phrase: *los gringos que caminan*—the *gringos* who walk.

Up and to the Right

Karl Johnson and I both graduated from Cornell University in 1990, though we never met during our undergraduate years. I moved away from Ithaca, New York, returning only to visit, but Karl stayed. There were two big things missing from his Cornell experience, and he wanted future students to have them. Amazingly enough, he's managed to build them both.

In 2000 Karl founded a Christian study center called Chesterton House, an intellectual, spiritual and residential community now based in a sprawling house on fraternity row.

But before he started Chesterton House, Karl built the other thing he thought Cornell was missing: a ropes course.

Tucked in the woods a ten-minute drive from the center of campus, there are trapeze bars high above the forest floor, balance beams fifty feet off the ground and a replica of Cornell's iconic bell tower at one end of a four-hundred-foot double zip-line. Students, corporate groups and the occasional team of Olympic-level gymnasts use the course to test their limits and build their trust. It's still Karl's baby, as you can tell from the careful way he coils every rope, and though he no longer works for Cornell's Outdoor Education program, he still has a key.

Late one summer afternoon, Karl's family met mine at the gate for some of the most terrifying risk-free moments of our lives.

This is the inside joke about ropes courses: they are about as far from real risk as you can get. Strapped into the expert-tested, lawyer-approved, triple-checked, over-engineered systems of harnesses and ropes that secure every maneuver, I was probably safer than I have ever been in my life.

But that sure isn't how it felt at the top of a thirty-foot pole, looking at a twelve-inch-square platform in front of my nose that I was supposed to somehow clamber onto and stand up on—and then jump. Jumping off seemed like the easy part. That would be an act of exhilarating authority, safeguarded by the harness around my chest. But getting even one foot onto that tiny platform—let alone both feet, let alone standing up, the pole swaying underneath me—that prospect created a perfect storm between my body's primal fear of falling and my mind's vivid anticipation of how embarrassing it would be to tumble off ignominiously in the attempt.

On the other hand, there was no way I was going to completely give up and slither back down the pole. I called down to Karl, holding the belay rope far below. "Maybe I'll just jump off now," I said.

"Well, you could do that," he responded in a perfectly even tone of voice. "But when is the next time you'll be on top of a pole like this? Why waste this chance? How about trying to just sit on the platform?"

I pondered my options—and, watching below, my wife. And my teenagers.

I pondered some more.

"I'll try," I said. My arms were trembling with adrenaline. Instructed by Karl, I managed to get halfway to a sitting position. Then he said, "You know, you're really close to being able to stand up. How about trying to get one foot all the way on the platform?"

I maneuvered one foot, just barely, into position. Karl's voice floated up again. "You're really close. I bet you can get your other foot up there." Sure enough, I could. Now, amazingly enough, I was squatting on the platform.

"I don't know if I can stand up," I said. I wished I had been keeping up on my squats and pistols, but on that high swaying pole, the issue was less strength than balance.

"You can," Karl said in a perfectly steady voice.

Now my legs were trembling, too. But inch by inch, more slowly than I've ever stood up in my life, I gradually raised myself all the way. Finally, I was standing on top of the platform. Karl's wife, Julie, took a picture. My wife and kids cheered. Then, with a roar of triumph and laughter, I leapt into thin air.

Our whole family made it to the top of the pole that day. Each one of us stopped where I had stopped, all but convinced we couldn't go on. With each one, Karl found a way to coach us past our fears, gradually increasing our authority, discerning and addressing our vulnerability. He was our security, the belay rope threaded through pulleys and wrapped around his waist, but he was also the one calling us to more risk than we thought we could bear.

Karl is a good leader, and he is also a good friend. Good leaders, and friends, increase our authority *and* vulnerability, even while they carefully assess how much authority and how much vulnerability we can stand. That late afternoon on the ropes course, our family learned something about leadership—and about discipleship. We had to follow Karl, who had built the course, inspected it, trained on it. He asked us to try nothing he had not tried, and to trust nothing he had not made trustworthy. We needed his voice from the forest floor, coaching us further than we could have gone. We needed someone who had already gone where he was asking us to go.

Judging by the smiles on all of our faces, and the endless retelling of the stories of our triumphs, falls and failures

over the weeks after our visit to the ropes course, what Karl
led us into was flourishing.

UNLOCKING TRUE AUTHORITY

> We needed someone who
> had already gone where he
> was asking us to go.

The ropes course was just
a game—a simulation of
real life, not the real thing. Gymnasts and circus performers
do everything we did and more, with no harness and no
nets. But the triple-tested security of the ropes course
makes visible the essential wager of the Christian life. Are
we ultimately vulnerable? Is everything at risk in this life
with no belays, no harnesses, no one holding the rope at
the other end? Or is our very life held by one who has gone
even to the dust of death and returned, who has conquered
the ultimate source of vulnerability, and even now holds
absolutely secure the tether of our life? If Christ is not
raised from the dead, then everything is at stake and at risk,
the gods of authority without vulnerability have won, and
we are of all people the most to be pitied. But if in fact
Christ has been raised—this is the wager of the Christian
life—then no meaningful risk is too great for his capacity
to rescue.

In the grip of idols, we believe that our problem is not
enough authority. Life becomes a quest to acquire enough
authority to manage and minimize our vulnerability. The

risks are all around us, obvious and endless—the terror of nature, the hostility of others, the inexorable approach of death. To people who see the world this way, gaining authority without vulnerability is the pearl of great price, something you would sell everything to obtain. And in the grip of idolatry and injustice, that is exactly what we do.

But from the first page to the last, the story that has turned the world upside down says our situation is actually exactly the reverse. Our problem isn't acquiring enough authority—not if we are truly made in the image of the world's all-powerful Creator, blessed with memory, reason and skill, the rulers of creation. If that was true of our beginning, it is all the more true of our future: "Do you not know that we are to judge angels?" Paul asks the Corinthians (1 Corinthians 6:3). Their pursuit of false power betrayed their misunderstanding of their true authority: "Let no one boast about human leaders. For all things are yours, whether Paul or Apollos or Cephas or the world or life or death or the present or the future—all belong to you, and you belong to Christ, and Christ belongs to God" (1 Corinthians 3:21-23).

Judging from Paul's later correspondence with them, the Corinthians didn't think much of this idea. They seem to have been easily infatuated with leaders who claimed spiritual power and backed it up with impressive personal appearances. Paul's long-suffering and often beleaguered ministry was far too visibly vulnerable. When he writes them again a few years later, even more grieved and exasperated than before, Paul is driven to the very edge of claiming exactly the sort of spiritual exceptionalism the Corinthians prized. But he is so unwilling to boast about it that he pretends he is speaking about someone else:

> I know a person in Christ who fourteen years ago was caught up to the third heaven—whether in the body or out of the body I do not know; God knows. And I know that such a person—whether in the body or out of the body I do not know; God knows—was caught up into Paradise and heard things that are not to be told, that no mortal is permitted to repeat. (2 Corinthians 12:2-4)

We have every reason to believe that Paul is in fact describing his own extraordinary spiritual experience here, exactly the sort of "visions and revelations from the Lord" that would have secured his spiritual authority in the fevered atmosphere of the Corinthian church. But something has happened to turn Paul's understanding of authority and vulnerability upside down:

> On behalf of such a one I will boast, but on my own behalf I will not boast, except of my weaknesses. But if I wish to boast, I will not be a fool, for I will be speaking the truth. But I refrain from it, so that no

one may think better of me than what is seen in me or heard from me, even considering the exceptional character of the revelations. Therefore, to keep me from being too elated, a thorn was given me in the flesh, a messenger of Satan to torment me, to keep me from being too elated. Three times I appealed to the Lord about this, that it would leave me, but he said to me, "My grace is sufficient for you, for power is made perfect in weakness." So, I will boast all the more gladly of my weaknesses, so that the power of Christ may dwell in me. Therefore I am content with weaknesses, insults, hardships, persecutions, and calamities for the sake of Christ; for whenever I am weak, then I am strong. (2 Corinthians 12:5-10)

We do not know exactly what the "thorn in the flesh" was that tormented Paul. But his choice of words is striking. A thorn stuck in one's flesh would be a constant source of, and reminder of, bodily weakness. But for someone who knew the story of Christ's final passion, it would also be a constant reminder of the sign of authority that had been placed on the head of Jesus on the way to the cross, the thorns that pressed into his head as he risked everything to restore the world to true flourishing.

We do not lack for authority. In Christ we have all the authority that we need and more—"all things are yours" (1 Corinthians 3:21). But what unlocks that authority is the willingness to expose ourselves to meaningful loss—to become vulnerable, woundable in the world. For this, too, is what it means to bear the divine image—if the One through whom all things were made spoke into being a world where he himself could be betrayed, wounded and killed. What we are missing, to become like him, is not ultimately more authority—it is more vulnerability.

This is why both of the distinctive callings of transformative people involve vulnerability, hidden and chosen. This is why the evidently vulnerable are such crucial parts of all of our flourishing—why my niece Angela is not just the object of our care but a subject in her own right, someone who draws out from us the capacity to be truly and fully human. This is why our hidden and obvious flaws, failures and limitations are in fact the path to true strength. This is the good news for everyone who feels too vulnerable and powerless to have real authority: in the upside-down economy of the Kingdom, you possess the pearl which everyone must seek. Like Paul, who discovered that his "thorn in the flesh" was in fact the path toward God's power being made perfect, you have with you, and within you, the secret of a life that unlocks true power.

INVITATIONS TO RISK

Pursue authority by itself and you will not only end up without the authority you seek but plunged into the very kind of vulnerability you hoped to avoid. But the reverse is not true. Because God is for us in our vulnerability, because "all things are ours," because even the ultimate vulnerability of death cannot hold us in its grip—the pursuit of vulnerability actually leads to authority and to the flourishing that comes when authority and vulnerability are combined.

I am reminded of this in my frequent conversations with students and emerging adults about their callings and careers. Understandably, the felt need of nearly every young person is how to acquire authority—how to gain the capacity to act in the workplace and in the broader world. And yet, my advice to them almost always comes down to this: embrace more risk. Only those who have opened themselves to meaningful risk are likely to be entrusted with the authority that we all were made for and seek. Indeed, to seek out meaningful risk actually is its own kind of act of authority, because in the economy of the world's true Creator and Redeemer, meaningful risk *is* the most meaningful action, the life that really is life, the flourishing for which we were created.

> Only those who have opened themselves to meaningful risk are likely to be entrusted with authority.

This does not mean, as the narrow sense of the word *vulnerability* might mislead us to think, that we all have to spend our lives quivering like emotional Jell-O. The invitation to risk takes many forms, and while some of them take us down and to the right, requiring the sacrifice that every leader must eventually make, many other forms place us squarely on the path to flourishing. When we lead with these kinds of vulnerability, we find the best kind of authority is given to us as well.

Accountability. In the most literal sense, we invite others to examine our "accounts"—to probe the records we keep and the stories we tell for signs of truth or falsehood. The best accountability runs a spectrum from daily honesty to expert scrutiny, "downward" to those with less power and "upward" to those with more. If we manage a business, we open its accounts both to the firm's own bookkeepers and to the gimlet eye of outside auditors who are expert in assessing financial statements. If we teach, we seek out the evaluations of our students, our peers and more experienced, wiser mentors. We embrace the kinds of community where our façades of competence can fall and we can be known in all our messy glory. We seek out friends who ask hard questions and then ask them again; we find confessors who will hear our account of our own sins and failings and offer us severe mercy rather than mushy indulgence.

Confrontation. Years ago I read of researchers who had followed a cohort of middle managers in an American firm over many years. Some of them advanced to senior levels in the firm, while others did not. What was the difference between these two groups? The researchers found only one significant difference: one group was consistently quicker than the other to speak up when something was going wrong in their area of responsibility. When they spotted impending failure, they grabbed anyone who would listen—coworkers, their boss, their boss's boss—and got them involved in figuring out what was going wrong and what could change. The other group tended to minimize potential failure, avert their eyes from warning signs and cover up the eventual damage.

Which managers ended up more "successful" in their careers? The ones who pretended everything was basically fine, telling others, and probably themselves, what they wanted to hear? No.

The ones who succeeded were the ones who failed loudly, quickly and boldly—rather than softly, slowly and timidly.

We pursue true vulnerability, the kind that leads to flourishing, when we use our authority to recognize and address failure rather than using our authority to conceal and minimize failure. We learn to speak up early when something feels wrong. To raise the possibility of

> The ones who succeeded were the ones who failed loudly, quickly and boldly—rather than softly, slowly and timidly.

failure is always a risk—but it is a risk that can actually increase, not diminish, our authority.

Delegation. We learn that the desire to control others is an idolatry that will not deliver what we seek and will certainly not lead to their flourishing. So we turn over power to others, giving them authority to act on their own behalf, to cultivate and create in their own right rather than just implementing our vision. We discover the joy of true power, which is to make room for others to act with authority. We measure our lives increasingly by what others have done—and received credit for—thanks to our advocacy. By exposing ourselves to the risk that others will fail us, we also open up the possibility that they will surprise and delight us with the flourishing they create.

Solitude, silence and fasting. Embracing the three most essential spiritual disciplines opens us to the deepest kind of risk: the risk of discovering who we really are, in all our flaws and confusion. Solitude forces us to step away from the continual affirmation of our authority by others; silence compels us to practice quietness rather than noisy self-assertion; fasting exposes our dependence on food and other good things to prop up our sense of agency and capacity. All of them, practiced regularly, will humble us, bringing us up against our own limits and our own foolishness. Without solitude, silence and fasting, we have no true authority—we are captives of others' approval, addicted to our personal soundtracks and chained to our pleasures. But on the other side of this vulnerability is true authority, grounded in something deeper than our circumstances.

TAKE A RISK EVERY NIGHT

The speaker's arrival had been keenly anticipated—the room was full and hushed as he stepped on stage. The message was masterfully delivered, with down-to-earth yet dramatic stories. There were memorable turns of phrase, well-honed principles and a few disarming personal disclosures.

And it all was strangely familiar—because I had heard it, down to every emotional catch in the throat and pregnant pause, delivered to a different audience nine months before.

Repetition and reproduction aren't bad things in themselves. Every copy of this book, after all, contains the exact same message, delivered in the same way to each reader. We sing songs over and over again, repeating the same lyrics and tunes until we have learned them by heart. As someone who speaks frequently to new audiences, I certainly appreciate the value of a well-crafted presentation, one that has been tested and tried many times before.

And yet on this particular evening, something felt off. Surely there had been some real vulnerability involved in the original writing, crafting and delivery of this talk. But that was months or years in the past. What risk was happening now, tonight, with this group of people gathered in hopes of hearing a true and transforming word? It was hard to see how such distant vulnerability could match the evident authority granted by the stage, the setting and even those self-deprecating anecdotes—not to mention the private plane that had brought him, at the conference's expense, to the meeting.

Some experiences like this lead to cynicism, a quick and jaded judgment on people with privilege and power. But this particular night, I felt something more spiritually beneficial—an overwhelming fear that I could easily end up in the same condition. Perhaps not with all of the same trappings of power and fame, but cocooned nonetheless in self-protective, safe repetition of the moves and words that had gained me whatever power I had.

So I started seeking out the people who have to find a way to repeat the same words night after night and yet make every repetition real: professional actors. In the months after my moment of conference déjà vu, I asked several actors how they kept their performances authentic even while delivering precisely the same well-rehearsed lines.

"Every performance, I ask myself what risk I'm going to take that night," one friend told me. "Some nights I focus on just one line and try to express a new emotion through it. Or I think about doing something new in a scene that is becoming predictable."

I called James, another friend who spent eight years acting in New York. He told me,

> Actors have to memorize our lines, but the goal is not to memorize *only* the words—the goal is to live the story out truthfully on stage, and we can't do that if we have already decided how we are going to act. Take a famous scene, one every actor and every audience member knows, like Romeo going into the tomb where he will discover Juliet, dead. The actor knows that she's dead, the audience knows that she's dead, but *Romeo* doesn't know. Romeo has to discover it every time. You have to enter the scene, dream your dreams, hope your hopes—and let the play crush them.

James spent years training to have authority as an actor. But every night he plays Romeo, he has to find a way to make Romeo's vulnerability his own.

DO YOUR HOMEWORK

I learned a very different lesson about public speaking from a man I'll call Terry, whose remarkable career in business had culminated with an assignment as CEO of a Fortune 500 company. Terry was an unusual figure for a CEO, quiet almost to the point of shyness. After years leading smaller, privately held firms, his new role required him to give speeches to auditoriums full of investors or managers. Intimidated by the public-speaking demands, he had sought out his pastor.

"Terry, it's easy," his pastor said. "You only have to do three things to be an effective public speaker. Do your homework, love your audience, and be yourself."

Do your homework—acquire the proper authority to address the topic at hand. *Love your audience*—open yourself up to their vulnerability, their fears and dreams,

> "Do your homework, love your audience, and be yourself."

their ambitions and failures, and see them for the image bearers they are, with their own authority and capacity. And then *be yourself*—bring your own authority and vulnerability together, in all your beloved incompleteness, in their presence. Like all the best maxims, it is both utterly simple and a life's work to fulfill.

Terry found that this simple framework gave him exactly what he needed to step into his new role. Before every speaking engagement, he would ask himself, *Have I done my homework?* Years of accommodating a learning disability had taught him how to master material through painstaking effort, so the answer was always yes. He could shift his attention to the central question, *Do I love this audience?* That became his primary focus in the hours or days before a speech—envisioning the particular people who would be in the room and tuning his mind and heart to what would serve them best. Then, when he walked on stage, he had just one assignment: to be himself. The anxiety that used to surround public speaking disappeared. In its place was the authority and vulnerability that has led his company to flourish.

I mentioned Terry's three-step framework to James, the actor. "Exactly," he said. "And I would add that to love your audience is actually to *need* something from your audience—to go out on stage knowing that if they don't meet you, give you what you need, you can't do what you came to do. Real love only exists where there is a mutual need."

Given his busy schedule, I am certain that Terry has to repeat and reuse material, just like the speaker I heard twice in the same year. For that matter, Terry, too, arrives at many of his engagements on a private plane. They are superficially similar in their status, wealth and position. But the demands of leadership that have made one of them more distant over time have made the other more present. The same pressures that have led one to retreat into his authority have led the other to open himself up in vulnerability—to need others, to ask for advice and to continue to learn.

I want to be like Terry. I want to be like Karl, Drew, Isabel and the others who have shown me what real authority and real vulnerability mean, the ones who have drawn me into true flourishing. Like Paul Farmer, I want to be a saint—to become part of the ultimate meaningful story, taking hold of the life that really is life.

The great news is that it is possible. Do your homework—prepare for authority. Love your neighbor, enough to need them, enough to know what they need—open yourself to vulnerability. And then be yourself—show up with all that you have and all that you are and all the truth of what you will never be.

LAUGHTER

The stories we tell our friends, and often tell ourselves, fall overwhelmingly into two categories: stories where we are the hero and stories where we are the victim.

Hero stories feature us overcoming great odds and fierce opposition, often with a note of righteous triumph thrown in for good measure. Sitting on planes, I've overheard a lot of hero stories as people settle into their seats and call their loved ones. They tell them how they beat the traffic, how they got the last spot in the overhead bins, how they persuaded an unwilling agent to upgrade them to first class. Sitting in college dining halls, I've heard stories of turning in papers just before the deadline after a brutal all-nighter.

Hero stories are authority stories—ways of signaling to our friends that we are lucky, good or both. They are always selective at best, exaggerated at worst.

Then there are victim stories, which of course are vulnerability stories. We describe being cut off by an aggressive driver in a luxury car, missing the flight because the security lines were so long, being stood up by the world's most horrible date.

The theme of victim stories is actually the same as the theme of hero stories: our own vindication in an unfair world. We are well-intentioned and undeserving of our fate, at the mercy of petty or cosmic conspiracies, too small for the forces arrayed against us.

Whether we tell hero or victim stories, we are constantly tempted to exaggerate. As I write this chapter, America's most prominent television news presenter has seen his career rocked by an untrue tale of barely surviving a helicopter crash after coming under fire in Afghanistan—a tale that managed to present him both as victim and as hero. (In fact, his helicopter was miles away from the incident he "misremembered.")

> Our true story is not really about us—it is about our rescuer.

But there is another kind of story we all could tell—a story that paints us in a very different light. It is a *rescue* story.

"I once was lost, but now am found"—that is no exaggeration. The more we grasp how truly we lost hold of our true calling, how completely we were in the grip of injustice, safety and poverty, the more we realize how great the rescue has been, how little we ourselves can claim for our own credit.

Our true story is not really about us—it is about our

rescuer. He arrives in our story and acts with authority—he is the true hero. And yet he also bears our vulnerability—he offers himself as the victim. His arrival in the story sets us free to flourish. And the mark of his arrival is not the hero's grim shout of triumph or the victim's grim cry of despair, but the distinctive sound of those surprised by joy: *laughter.*

> When the Lord restored the fortunes of Zion,
>   we were like those who dream.
> Then our mouth was filled with laughter,
>   and our tongue with shouts of joy;
> then it was said among the nations,
>   "The Lord has done great things for them."
>   (Psalm 126:1-2)

If you want one last picture of authority and vulnerability together, laughter will do the trick. To laugh, to really laugh out loud, is to be vulnerable, taken beyond ourselves, overcome by surprise and gratitude. And to really laugh may be the last, best kind of authority—the capacity to see the meaning of the whole story and discover that our final act, our only enduring responsibility in that story, is simply celebration, delight and worship.

> If you want one last picture of authority and vulnerability together, laughter will do the trick.

After we have borne our hidden vulnerability, even after we have descended to the dead, after we have been rescued from our suffering, our withdrawing, our exploiting—we will be raised up, restored to our rightful place. And we will laugh.

THE LIFE THAT REALLY IS LIFE

The summer I finish this book brings my parents' fiftieth wedding anniversary. We converge on their rambling house in Massachusetts for a simple celebration that begins at church on Sunday morning and continues on the large screened porch that faces the woods in their backyard. The cousins—my sisters' children and mine—gather to play music and games. In our midst is Angela, almost eleven years old.

I would never want to romanticize in the slightest the great burden Angela has placed on my sister's family, how much caring for her has cost them in every possible currency—sleep, freedom, finances, personal health. On the worst nights, deep in the winter darkness of northern New England, on the rushed and anxious drives to the hospital for yet another baffling change in her condition—dealing every day with the literal weight of a human being who requires every kind of care but cannot care for herself—Angela has exposed them to deeper vulnerability than any of us would choose for ourselves. The only way the burden has been even remotely bearable has come as others have chosen vulnerability as well—my parents' innumerable trips up and down the long highway between their homes, the checks we all have written toward special equipment and supplies, the friends who relieved my sister for a few hours just when it seemed the tedium and challenge of constant attendance to Angela's needs were too much, the community, state and nation that provide programs to support families like hers.

With Angela in our midst, with all her inescapable vulnerability, something profoundly healthy has happened in my family of origin, a family where love has been real but also has been tested and sometimes has been all too hard. Scattered across three states, distracted by the demands and opportunities of fruitful work and the countless distractions of the thin, virtual world, we—maybe the more honest word is *I*—could easily have missed the call to flourish together. But Angela has concentrated our attention and our love. In a centrifugal world where everything and everyone flees the demands of love, Angela was a center of gravity, drawing us back to one another and to true life—the life that really is life, the life that money cannot buy: the life of making flourishing possible, at great cost and with great tears.

She could never know it, but Angela's whole life was only possible because of an ever-widening web of extraordinary acts of love and sacrifice, authority and vulnerability.

Of course, the same is true for every one of us.

On a summer day like this one, on a blanket with simple toys in reach, the sun on her hair and breeze in her face, Angela is flourishing. She is known, she is loved, and because she exists, others are called up and to the right with her.

She has the only life worth having—the life that really is life. And because of her, the rest of us do, too.

As this book was being prepared for publication, Angela Frances Ricker died at home of complications from her condition. She was eleven years old. She died, as she was born and as she lived, surrounded by love.

ACKNOWLEDGMENTS

My deepest thanks to my parents, Wayne and Joyce, for their firmness and their warmth in my childhood and for their generosity and openness in my adulthood, and to Melinda and Dave Ricker for showing me in so many ways what love and flourishing can be.

Editors and agents, too, create flourishing when they combine authority and vulnerability. Thank you to Andy Le Peau for proving that it is possible—and necessary—to be both feared and loved! This book is so much better for his unflinching honesty and his unbending patience. Thank you to Kathy Helmers for her invaluable contributions to the shaping of this book and its argument.

To the whole InterVarsity Press team, not least to Cindy Kiple for yet another pitch-perfect cover—thank you for taking mere words and making them available in such artful ways to so many readers.

My wife, Catherine, is my first and best reader, the one who knows and shares my authority and vulnerability, and the greatest gift of flourishing in my life. Thank you.

Notes

Chapter 1: Beyond the False Choice

pp. 15-16 *Firmness and warmth, it turns out:* The vast literature on these two dimensions of "parenting style," which was an organizing principle of Diana Baumrind's work, converges on Maccoby and Martin's 1983 review article, "Socialization in the Context of the Family: Parent-Child Interaction," in P. H. Mussen and E. M. Hetherington, *Handbook of Child Psychology: Vol. 4. Socialization, Personality, and Social Development,* 4th ed. (New York: John Wiley & Sons, 1983). It is summarized in accessible form online, with further references, at Kendra Cherry's "Parenting Styles: The Four Styles of Parenting," http://psychology.about.com/od/developmentalpsychology/a/parenting-style.htm. It is important to note that one ongoing area of research and debate is how widely Baumrind's categories apply outside the dominant culture of North America. See the discussion in Nancy Darling and Laurence Steinberg, "Parenting Style as Context: An Integrative Model," *Psychological Bulletin* 113, no. 3 (1993), 487-96.

p. 16 *being nice and being kind:* Thanks to Kelly Monroe Kullberg (in another context) for this lovely and insightful distinction.

p. 17 *quadrants:* Apologies to math whizzes, for whom my numbering goes the wrong direction—and who will also notice that this is not really a proper coordinate system.

Chapter 2: Flourishing

p. 30 *Angela:* My brother-in-law David Ricker wrote about Angela's early months in "Trisomy 13," *Lifelines* (2011-2012), 66-74, available at http://geiselmed.dartmouth.edu/lifelines/pdf/2012_lifelines.pdf.

p. 35 *Think of authority this way:* In what follows I have been helped tremendously by Oliver O'Donovan (especially *The Desire of the Nations: Rediscovering the Roots of Political Theology* [New York: Cambridge University Press, 1999]), Victor Austin (*Up with Authority: Why We Need Authority to Flourish* *as Human Beings* [New York: T&T Clark, 2010]), and most recently, David T. Koyzis, (*We Answer to Another: Authority, Office, and the Image of God* [Eugene, OR: Pickwick, 2014]). Koyzis is especially comprehensive and clarifying. While I omit many of his valuable distinctions in this simple discussion, I recommend his book as the first stop for anyone looking for a treatment of authority from a Christian perspective and as a next step for those who have read my book *Playing God* into the nuances of political theory and its implications for flourishing communities and institutions.

p. 39 *The sorrow of the whole human story:* Many others have stated this idea before me, including, as David T. Koyzis notes, Richard T. De George in *The Nature and Limits of Authority*: "The enemy, however, is not authority but the abuse of authority" (quoted in Koyzis, 171).

p. 42 *The very first word:* Patrick Lencioni, *Getting Naked: A Business Fable About Shedding the Three Fears That Sabotage Client Loyalty* (San Francisco: Jossey-Bass, 2010).

pp. 44-45 *Indeed, as the scholar:* Walter Brueggemann, "Of the Same Flesh and Bone," *Catholic Biblical Quarterly*, vol. 32 (1970), 532-42. I was alerted to this article by a blog post by Matthew Lee Anderson.

p. 46 *As I was writing this chapter the makers:* "Days of My Youth," https://youtube/aDEaAOcDKnA, accessed July 6, 2015.

CHAPTER 3: SUFFERING

p. 64 *the dirty work every social media company must somehow handle:* Adrian Chen, "The Laborers Who Keep Dick Pics and Beheadings Out of Your Facebook Feed," *Wired* (October 2014). Accessed online at www.wired.com/2014/10/content-moderation/. As the title indicates, the article contains graphic descriptions (though not images) of highly disturbing online content.

p. 67 *a district in India where bonded labor—modern-day child slavery—had been endemic:* I described this visit in more detail in *Playing God* (Downers Grove, IL: InterVarsity Press, 2013), 19-24.

CHAPTER 4: WITHDRAWING

p. 84 *a bigger industry than movies:* Gartner, Inc., "Gartner Says Worldwide Video Game Market to Total $93 Billion in 2013," www.gartner.com/newsroom/

id/2614915, accessed February 21, 2015. PwC, "Global entertainment and media outlook 2015-2019," www.pwc.com/gx/en/global-entertainmentmedia-outlook/segment-insights/filmed-entertainment.jhtml, accessed February 21, 2015.

p. 88 *milking a cow in* Minecraft: "Farming Sheep, Cows and Pigs in Minecraft," www.minecraft101.net/g/farming-animals.html, accessed December 31, 2014.

CHAPTER 5: EXPLOITING

p. 100 *Phil and Leslie:* Phil Bowling-Dyer wrote about this experience in "Being Black in Our Neighborhood—and in America," *re:generation quarterly* (Spring 2001), available at www.ctlibrary.com/rq/2001/spring/7108.html, accessed July 6, 2015.

CHAPTER 6: HIDDEN VULNERABILITY

p. 123 *thirty thousand commercial plane flights in the United States every day:* Jad Mouawad and Christopher Drew, "Airline Industry at Its Safest Since the Dawn of the Jet Age," *The New York Times*, 11 February 2013, page A1 (available at www.nytimes.com/2013/02/12/business/2012-was-the-safest-year-for-airlines-globally-since-1945.html, accessed February 21, 2015).

p. 132 *Ted Haggard in a hotel room:* The image accompanied the cover story, "Good Morning, Evangelicals!," *Christianity Today*, November 2005.

CHAPTER 7: DESCENDING TO THE DEAD

p. 149 *"It was the spring semester of the academic year, and I was in trouble":* Philip Ryken, "Nobody Knows the Trouble I've Seen," available online at www.youtube.com/watch?v=_yVQ8xVp7kA, accessed February 19, 2015.

p. 156 *Steve Hayner:* The story of Steve and Sharol's journey through his months with cancer is told in *Joy in the Journey: Finding Abundance in the Shadow of Death* (Downers Grove, IL: InterVarsity Press, 2015).

CHAPTER 8: UP AND TO THE RIGHT

p. 168 *blessed with memory, reason and skill, the rulers of creation:* This language is adapted from Eucharistic Prayer C in the Book of Common Prayer of The Episcopal Church.

p. 173 *a cohort of middle managers in an American firm over many years:* Unfortunately I cannot recover the article that described this study.

DISCUSSION GUIDE

1. Crouch defines *flourishing* as being fully alive, connected to our own human purpose as well as somehow participating in the glory of God. How would you define *flourishing*? What does it look like to you?

2. What do you think of Crouch's paradox that flourishing comes from being both strong and weak?

3. How is Jesus, being both strong and weak, an example of flourishing?

4. How did you respond to the story of Angela in chapter two, someone profoundly disabled who nonetheless had a profound effect on those around her?

5. Suffering can be physical, financial, emotional, social and spiritual. We all visit the quadrant of Suffering (chap. 3). What are the short-term and long-term effects of suffering on people?

6. Crouch says building lasting authority is essential to lift both individuals and communities out of suffering. Do you agree or not? Explain.

7. In chapter four Crouch says safety is a good thing, where we hopefully all start in life. Why can clinging to the quadrant of Withdrawing actually be debilitating for human beings?

8. The real temptation for most of us is not complete apathy, but activities that simulate meaningful action and meaningful risk without actually asking much of us or transforming much in us. Crouch mentions cruises and video

games as examples. He also discusses small, practical steps that could move us out of the quadrant of Withdrawing, like turning off electronic devices for a while or asking a friend questions just one step deeper than usual. What are concrete ways you could take a step out of the Withdrawing quadrant?

9. In chapter five Crouch says Exploiting is seeking to avoid vulnerability by increasing our authority. The best early warning sign that we are drifting toward Exploiting (in work or family relationships, in addictions from alcohol to romance novels) is that our closest relationships begin to decay. Do you think this is true or not? Explain.

10. Which of the three quadrants (Suffering, Withdrawing, Exploiting) do you find yourself in most often and why?

11. Crouch offers two ways to move toward Flourishing, two ways exemplified by Jesus. The first, in chapter six, is that of hidden vulnerability. Do you agree that sometimes it is necessary to hide our vulnerabilities so others can flourish? Explain.

12. Crouch says that no one survives hidden vulnerability without companions who understand. How have you found that to be true?

13. What do you think of Crouch's contention in chapter seven, "Descending to the Dead," that only as we embrace suffering from a position of authority can we find true flourishing?

14. What are some practical ways to lay aside authority (become vulnerable) so others can take it up and bring flourishing?

15. What is the key, the most helpful idea, you take away from *Strong and Weak*?

Also by Andy Crouch

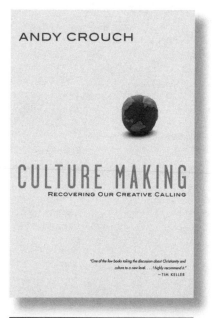

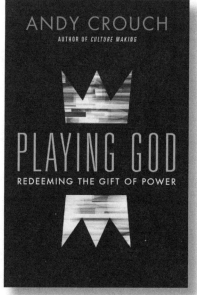

THE IVP SIGNATURE COLLECTION

Since 1947 InterVarsity Press has been publishing thoughtful Christian books that serve the university, the church, and the world. In celebration of our seventy-fifth anniversary, IVP is releasing special editions of select iconic and bestselling books from throughout our history.

RELEASED IN 2019

Basic Christianity (1958)
JOHN STOTT

How to Give Away Your Faith (1966)
PAUL E. LITTLE

RELEASED IN 2020

The God Who Is There (1968)
FRANCIS A. SCHAEFFER

This Morning with God (1968)
EDITED BY CAROL ADENEY AND BILL WEIMER

The Fight (1976)
JOHN WHITE

Free at Last? (1983)
CARL F. ELLIS JR.

The Dust of Death (1973)
OS GUINNESS

The Singer (1975)
CALVIN MILLER

RELEASED IN 2021

Knowing God (1973)
J. I. PACKER

Out of the Saltshaker and Into the World
(1979) REBECCA MANLEY PIPPERT

A Long Obedience in the Same Direction
(1980) EUGENE H. PETERSON

More Than Equals (1993)
SPENCER PERKINS AND CHRIS RICE

Between Heaven and Hell (1982)
PETER KREEFT

Good News About Injustice (1999)
GARY A. HAUGEN

The Challenge of Jesus (1999)
N. T. WRIGHT

Hearing God (1999)
DALLAS WILLARD

RELEASED IN 2022

The Heart of Racial Justice (2004)
BRENDA SALTER McNEIL AND
RICK RICHARDSON

Sacred Rhythms (2006)
RUTH HALEY BARTON

Habits of the Mind (2000)
JAMES W. SIRE

True Story (2008)
JAMES CHOUNG

Scribbling in the Sand (2002)
MICHAEL CARD

The Next Worship (2015)
SANDRA MARIA VAN OPSTAL

Delighting in the Trinity (2012)
MICHAEL REEVES

Strong and Weak (2016)
ANDY CROUCH

Liturgy of the Ordinary (2016)
TISH HARRISON WARREN

IVP SIGNATURE BIBLE STUDIES

As companions to the IVP Signature Collection, IVP Signature Bible Studies feature the inductive study method, equipping individuals and groups to explore the biblical truths embedded in these books.

Basic Christianity Bible Study
JOHN STOTT

How to Give Away Your Faith Bible Study
PAUL E. LITTLE

The Singer Bible Study, CALVIN MILLER

Knowing God Bible Study, J. I. PACKER

A Long Obedience in the Same Direction Bible Study, EUGENE H. PETERSON

Good News About Injustice Bible Study
GARY A. HAUGEN

Hearing God Bible Study
DALLAS WILLARD

The Heart of Racial Justice Bible Study
BRENDA SALTER McNEIL AND
RICK RICHARDSON

True Story Bible Study, JAMES CHOUNG

The Next Worship Bible Study
SANDRA MARIA VAN OPSTAL

Strong and Weak Bible Study
ANDY CROUCH